CNBC
Guide to
Money and
Markets

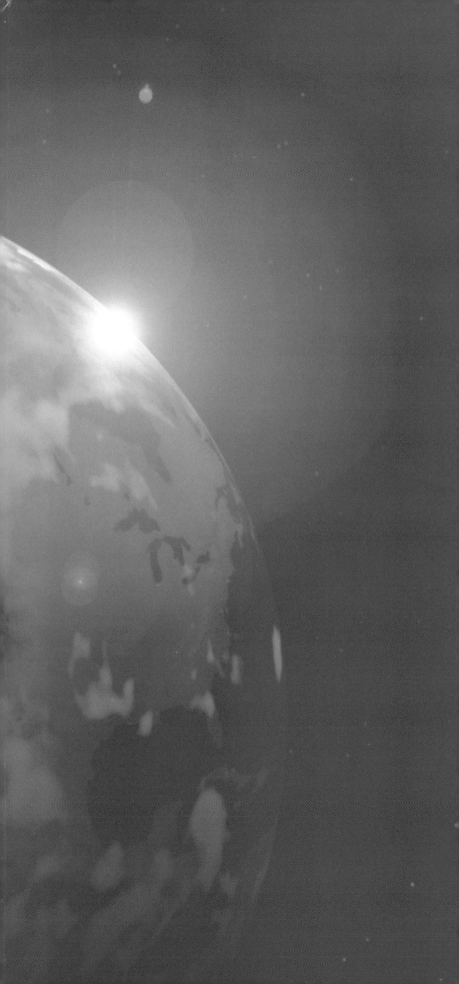

CNBC Guide to Money and Markets

Everything You Need to Know About Your Finances and Investments

CNBC with Jeff Wuorio

John Wiley & Sons, Inc.

CADER BOOKS

About the Authors

CNBC is the recognized global leader in business news, providing real-time financial market coverage and business information to more than 175 million homes and offices worldwide.

Jeff Wuorio is a longtime personal financial journalist and author. His work has appeared in *Money Magazine, The New York Times News Service, Business Week, Microsoft MoneyCentral* and other publications and web sites. His prior book, *Got Money? Enjoy it, Manage it — Even Save Some of it — Financial Advice for Your Twenties and Thirties,* was published in 1999.

This book is printed on acid-free paper.

Cover and book design by Charles Kreloff

ISBN: 0-471-39993-0

Printed in the United States of America.

10 9 8 7 6 5 4 3 2 1

Contents

Introduction 9

General Planning

Investment Goals 12
Putting a Plan Together 14
Other Investment Factors 16
Some Sample Portfolios 18

Stocks

Stocks: Your Share of the Pie 20
Stock Types 22
Choosing Stocks: The Basics 24
Inside the Financial Statement 26
More Ways to Evaluate Stocks 28
Other Stock Analyses 30
Special Strategies 32
How to Buy Stock 34
Other Ways to Buy Stock 36
More Ways to Buy—Initial Public Offerings 38
Trading by Insiders 40

Bonds

Bond Basics 42
Breaking Down Bonds 44
How Bonds Work 46
The Risks of Bonds 48
How to Buy and Track Bonds 50

Funds

Mutual Funds—An Introduction 52
Stock Funds—Part One 54

Types of Stock Funds—Part Two 56
More Stock Funds 58
Choosing a Mutual Fund 60
More Issues to Consider 62
Some Final Mutual Fund Issues 64
How to Buy a Mutual Fund 66
Tracking Your Mutual Funds 68
Other Mutual Funds—Bond Funds 70
How to Choose a Bond Fund 72
Money Market Mutual Funds 74

Other Investments

Certificates of Deposit 76
Individual Retirement Accounts—Part One 78
Individual Retirement Accounts—Part Two 80
Choosing the Right IRA 82
Other Types of IRAs 84
401ks—An Overview 86
Employee Stock Options 88

Getting Help

Places to Find Help 90
More Places to Find Help 92
Other Places to Find Help 94
After-Hours Trading 96
International Investing 98
Day Trading 100
Another Place to Find Help 102

Commodities

Commodities 104
Commodities and Options 106
More on Commodities 108

Financial Basics

Budgeting Investment Goals 110
Digging Out of Credit Card Debt 112

Buying a Home 114
Saving for College 116
Life Insurance 118
Health Insurance 120
Homeowners Insurance 122
Other Types of Insurance 124

Frequently Asked Questions

Planning and Goals 126
Bonds 128
Mutual Funds 130
Money Market Funds and Certificates of Deposit 132
IRAs, 401ks, and Stock Options 134
Brokers, Planners, and Financial Software 136
After-Hours Trading, International Investing, and
        Buybacks 138
Futures and Options 140
Investment and Money Management 142
Retirement Accounts and Banking 144

Glossary 146

Index 169

Introduction

Financial guidance has never been more valuable than in the aftermath of the attacks of September 11, 2001. The events of that day, the war in Afghanistan and incidents of bioterrorism in the U.S. and abroad pushed the economy into a tailspin and roiled financial markets. What should individuals do to safeguard their money and prepare for the future? What do we need to know to ride out these challenging times?

CNBC prides itself on providing real-time, authoritative information. Its coverage enlightens and informs the sophisticated and novice investor alike. CNBC's GUIDE TO MONEY AND MARKETS is a guide for everyone, especially if you want to become more comfortable with your finances. It provides useful perspectives for these uncertain days and offers solid advice for those starting out on the investment path.

Although the stock market is a key focus, there's more to managing your money. You must first measure your risk tolerance, set some short- and long-term goals, understand how the various investment vehicles work, and more. Only then will you be prepared to focus on something as specific as the stock ticker.

There's lots of information in this book about stocks and mutual funds—and how the equity markets work. However, if you're not quite ready to dip into stocks, or want to inject more caution into your portfolio, you can learn about safer investments like Treasury securities, Municipal bonds and Certificates of Deposit.

If you're approaching retirement, then you'll want to read about investment strategies that will help you protect your nest egg. On the other hand, if you've just started working, you may need help putting together an appropriate portfolio that will take advantage of your lengthy investment horizon.

The world of investing has gotten more complex—the Internet and other technological advances have forced investors to follow and react to information faster than ever. In order for you to keep up with all of this, you'll first need to have a good understanding of the basics of money and markets. This guide will provide you with a firm foundation upon which you can build your future.

Having a financial strategy—for your future, for your children and for your family—is essential. We hope this Guide will make it easier for you to start setting your goals or help you fine tune the investment plans you already have.

CNBC
Guide to
Money and
Markets

Investment Goals

It may be surprising, but many people dive headfirst into investing without having a clear understanding of what they specifically want to accomplish. A carefully focused analysis of what you wish to achieve is absolutely essential when it comes to figuring out the sorts of investments and strategies that will work best in your situation. Have a look at three types of common investment goals. Answer each question in turn to help you get a better feel for your specific goals and what you may need to do to achieve them.

Three Types of Goals

Retirement

Whether you see yourself sunning on a balmy South Sea island or hauling your grandkids to every amusement park in sight, bear in mind that retirement is an expensive proposition. Here's an illustration: if you're 22 years old now, making $50,000 a year at your first job and planning to retire at age 65, you're going to need about $640,000 to retire on a $50,000 yearly income (not so exorbitant, by the way). Bear in mind, too, that this projection is for a single person with relatively modest wants—add a family or more expensive tastes, and the price tag jumps.

Consider these questions as you begin to get a feel for the goal of retirement and what it might take to get there:

▶ What does retirement mean to you (travel, financial security, an intact estate for your heirs)?

▶ How much do you think you'll need to reach those goals?

▶ How long until you retire?

▶ How much have you already set aside for retirement?

▶ How much will you be able to regularly save for retirement?

College

This is another big-ticket item and is becoming more so all the time. The average yearly cost of college as of 2001 is about $21,000, but that figure is slightly misleading. Ivy League and other competitive schools have sprinted past the $30,000-a-year mark and, on average, are going up at least several percentage points a year. State universities, those former bastions of affordability, now routinely cost more than $10,000 a year.

If those figures put images of truck-driving school into your head for Junior, don't despair quite yet. By starting early and planning

How Secure?

When planning for retirement, should you count on Social Security? Some in the government fear that the funds will be depleted as the baby boom generation enters retirement. The American public is mostly split on the issue. So it makes sense to work up retirement projections with and without Social Security.

Define Your Long-term Goals as

carefully, you can, at the very least, take a good chunk out of those expenses. But, first, mull over these issues:

▶ How many kids will likely go to college?

▶ How old are your kids now?

▶ What sort of school do you think they'll attend, public or private?

▶ How much have you saved so far?

▶ How much will you be able to regularly save for college?

Housing

No surprise here, but the cost of housing has skyrocketed in recent years. For instance, the average cost of a three-bedroom home in both San Francisco and Boston now exceeds a half a million dollars. Granted, most other places are a good deal less expensive (Baltimore, by comparison, checks in at a modest $150,000 or so), but buying a home is still likely to be the single largest financial commitment that most of us will make in our lives.

The difference, of course, between a home and other big-ticket items is that, unless you have a grove of money trees out back, you don't simply pay for a home. Instead, the questions boil down to how much it will cost to get into the home of your choice and, thereafter, how much you can reasonably afford in mortgage payments, property taxes and other expenses. So, here are some issues along those lines:

▶ How large a home do you need?

▶ How large a home can you afford (monthly payments, property taxes, upkeep, etc.)?

▶ When do you want to buy your home?

▶ How long do you expect to stay in this home?

▶ What have you saved so far?

▶ How much do you think you'll be able to save regularly?

Calculated Help

Now that you've tackled these broad issues, it's time to start working on some real numbers. To do that, check out some of the online financial calculators listed below. These handy calculators let you play with all sorts of variables, including return and the time frame of your investments, to let you see how much major expenses are going to cost. Even better, you'll be taking the first step toward reaching these important lifetime goals.

Retirement

CNBC on MSN Money has a number of great calculators designed to help you work the numbers on a variety of issues impacting retirement. You can estimate your expenses at retirement, factor in the effects of inflation, and determine whether you're setting aside enough money for retirement. Visit http://moneycentral.msn.com/planning/home.asp

College

The College Board Online has a very handy calculator to help you determine whether you're setting enough aside for college. The calculator also lets you account for such variables as return on investments and money saved on a regular basis—that way, you get a feel for what you may need to adjust to hit your goals. Check it out at http://cbweb10p.collegeboard.org/finaid/fastud/html/fincalc/save.html

Housing

Home Advisor at CNBC on MSN Money serves up many calculators that let you address a variety of issues having to do with the cost of getting into (and keeping) your home. You can get a feel for closing costs, down payments, and other expenses, which will, in turn, give you a solid idea of the investment program you need to put together. They're at http://homeadvisor.msn.com/financing/financingoverview.asp

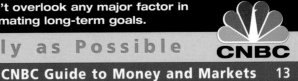

▲ Take a long-range view with long-term investing goals.

▼ Don't overlook any major factor in estimating long-term goals.

Specifically as Possible

Putting a Plan Together

Identifying your investment goals is really only the first step in devising an investment strategy. You also need to get a handle on such topics as the investments you should select, diversification, the effects of time on your investments, and other components of an investment strategy.

Some Things You Need to Know

Investment Choices

There are any number of choices you can make when devising an investment plan. They include **stocks, bonds, mutual funds, money market funds,** and **options** among others. Which ones you choose—and in what sort of balance—is dictated not only by your investment goals but also by other elements we'll discuss in this section of the book, including diversification, time, and how much risk you feel comfortable taking on.

Diversification

This is a somewhat mercurial term, but the concept essentially calls for spreading your money around among various types of investments such as stocks, bonds, and cash. The idea is to maximize your investment opportunities—for instance, historically bonds drop in value when stocks go up and vice versa—while limiting your exposure to losses (again, if you're taking a beating in bonds, your stocks have a decent chance of holding up).

Risk Tolerance

This is an element that you need to pay particularly close attention to—not only can it dictate what sort of investing success you enjoy, it also affects how happy (or miserable) you may be along the way.

Carefully evaluate how risky you want your investments to be. Will you be able to ride out market downturns with an aggressive stock or mutual fund in hopes of a big profit later, or would you prefer something a bit more solid and steady? Risk is also dictated by your goals and investing time frame, but your investments should also match who you are. Choosing something that doesn't fit may not only make you a nervous wreck, it can also ruin your investment strategy (with an aggressive stock, there's no more disastrous move than to sell when the price hits

Compound Power

Interested in a stark illustration of the power of compounding? Buying a stock in 1928 for $100 sounds like a bad idea, right? After all, a year later the stock market crashed and we hit the Great Depression. Well, if you had just left that stock on its own, by historical standards it would have earned about 12 percent a year. That means, by the turn of the century, your $100 "mistake" would be worth about three-quarters of a million dollars.

Time, Diversification, and Risk Are Central

bottom, something you may do if you're not comfortable with the risk).

Compounding

This term—more commonly associated with banking—also plays into investing so it is an important one to understand. Look at compounding in terms of "earnings from earnings." When you invest $100 at 10 percent interest a year, you get $110 at year's end. Leave that for another year at 10 percent and you end up with $121. From there, each year's earnings get steadily bigger the more compounding adds to the original amount. The same holds true with any investment you make—the longer you leave it and the more interest compounds, the greater your return.

Time and Risk

It's tempting to look at risk in a vacuum, but time is one factor that can greatly mitigate your investment risk. Statistics show that, in any given year, mutual funds have anywhere from a one-in-three to one-in-four chance of losing money. But, if you leave the money in for five years, your overall chance of losing drops to 4 percent. If you look at ten years, the likelihood of taking a loss becomes even smaller. This illustrates what we point out in other areas of this book—the longer the time frame, the less your chance of taking a loss (and, in turn, the greater the argument for a more aggressive strategy that has the chance to ride out market drops).

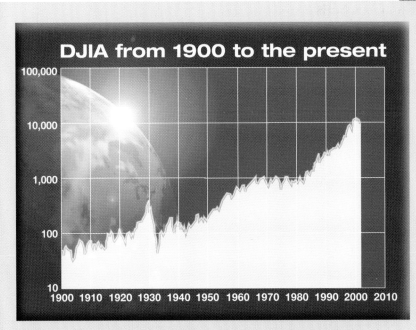

DJIA from 1900 to the present

To get an idea about the power of time and its effect on investment, have a look at the long-term growth of the Dow Jones Industrial Average. As you can see, the index—and the United States—have weathered some nasty times, but overall, the long-term trend has always been up.

▲ Diversification and time work to your financial benefit.

▼ Don't go against your nature when making financial decisions.

to Solid Investment Planning

CNBC

Other Investment Factors

Elements such as your goals and the time frame aren't the only influences on the success or failure of your investment strategy. There are several outside factors that, taken as a group or individually, can also carry a major impact, so it pays to know just what they are.

Major Outside Influences

Inflation

Inflation is one of the biggest headaches for investors, and unlike other problems, it creeps up on you years down the line. Inflation represents the erosion of the value of your money. For instance, with an annual inflation rate of 3 percent, $1 effectively buys only 97 cents worth of goods or services at the end of the year. Even worse, over a period of 10 years, that buck only gets you 70 cents worth of stuff.

So taking inflation into account is an important consideration when calculating your goals, especially long-term ones such as retirement or college planning for a young child. Many people dutifully invest for years, only to reach their goal to find that inflation has effectively taken a huge chunk out of their nest egg.

As we touched on in the discussion of planning—and will do more so in greater detail in the sample portfolio section—inflation means you need to be aggressive enough with your investment strategy to keep your purchasing power intact. Again, that doesn't mean going completely against your nature, but being too timid with your investments can be just as dangerous as being too aggressive.

Market Volatility

If you liken inflation to a slow oil leak in your car that only causes problems after a week or two, market volatility is the broken suspension that bounces you around every time you get behind the wheel. Market volatility—the everyday movement of the stock market—can be the most unsettling outside influence for many investors. For one thing, it's not a whole lot of fun watching your investments drop in value. Even if they bounce back and recover, the ups and downs of normal market flux can be enough to drive an investor to bury his money in the backyard and be done with it.

Market volatility goes back to

The Worldview

Of course there are other influences than the three listed above. One you may need to take into account is political stability around the world. So, if you own international stocks or mutual funds, know the countries where your money is going—if there's any political or social upheaval, that may impact your investments.

the discussion of risk tolerance. It's essential that you know your risk tolerance so that you have the temperament to weather market bounces of all kinds. And that also harkens back to your need to focus on long-term goals. Without that focus, you may panic during a market drop and do something you may ultimately regret.

Interest Rates

You are probably well acquainted with Alan Greenspan and his power over interest rates. Greenspan, chairman of the Federal Reserve, can raise and lower interest rates to stimulate or slow the economy. When rates fall, stock and bond prices rise while bond yields fall. When rates rise, bond yields recover while stock and bond prices head south.

The power of interest rates may not be obvious at first, but their movement does have a very real effect on your investments. Why do stocks go up when rates go down? One reason is that falling bond yields make stocks a comparatively more attractive investment. (Of course, the opposite is also true.)

The power of interest rates is not absolute or instant. For example, in 2001, multiple interest rate cuts failed to stop the economy from heading into a recession and the stock market from entering a bear market.

This points out the importance of diversification. When devising an investment strategy, it's essential that you spread your risk accordingly. Precisely how you do that depends on your goals and other considerations, but it's essential to diversify so, at the very least, not everything you have is going to take a hit at the same time.

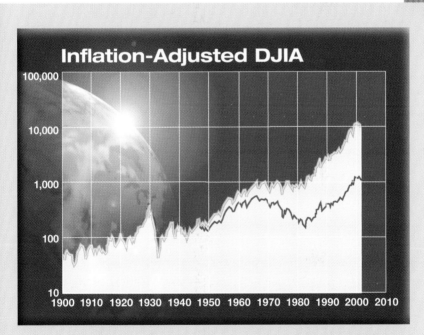

Inflation-Adjusted DJIA

Remember the chart we showed earlier that illustrated how the Dow Jones Industrial Average has gone up over the last century? Here's one that shows that, plus the effects of inflation (represented by the red line that breaks away from the upper line in the mid 1940s). It illustrates just how much inflation reduces the value of money, even with an investment as profitable as stocks over the long term.

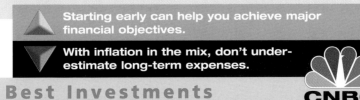

▲ Starting early can help you achieve major financial objectives.

▼ With inflation in the mix, don't underestimate long-term expenses.

the Best Investments

CNBC

Some Sample Portfolios

Having examined some of the issues involved in identifying investment goals and other considerations in putting together an investment strategy, we can now have a look at how all those factors come together in some sample portfolios. Before that, though, we'll look at the importance of diversification and, in turn, how that translates into the concept known as asset allocation.

Diversification, Hence Asset Allocation

Diversification means spreading your money among various sorts of investments to limit risk and maximize growth potential. While there are any number of places to invest, for most investors diversification breaks down into three different categories—stocks (or stock mutual funds), bonds (or bond mutual funds), and some form of cash, such as money market accounts, savings accounts, and money market funds.

Unto itself, this mix offers a degree of diversification. On the one hand, stocks generally offer the greatest potential for growth and profit for the investor; on the other, they generally carry the greatest amount of risk. By contrast, bonds are usually not considered as risky as stocks, nor do they offer their profit potential. The third element—cash, in some form—generally is virtually risk-free, but its returns are commensurately small. By combining these three elements, an investor takes advantage of growth potential—principally through stock holdings—while offsetting stocks' risk through more stable bonds and cash holdings.

If you're properly diversified, you're using a system known as asset allocation. In essence, this takes the three basic elements of stocks, bonds, and cash and divvies them up, taking into account such factors as your risk tolerance, your goals, your investing time frame, and other considerations.

If, for instance, you are a relatively aggressive investor—one willing to take on a fair amount of risk for the opportunity to reap big gains—one possible asset allocation would be 80 percent stocks, 10 percent bonds, and 10 percent cash. This sort of aggressive mix might also be suitable for an investor with a long-term goal, such as retirement, since there is ample time to weather downturns in the market.

A somewhat less aggressive breakdown might be 60 to 65 percent in stocks, 20 percent in bonds, and 15 to 20 percent in

Safe Money

First things first. Outside of the money you have to invest, be sure to set aside an emergency fund that's equal to as much as six months' living expenses. That protects you from the unexpected, ranging from loss of a job to a trip to the hospital. Put the money in a safe money-market account, as these are funds you don't want to gamble.

Asset Allocation Provides a Diversified

Investment Scenarios

Retirement

YEARS LEFT	INVESTMENT STYLE	ASSET ALLOCATION
More than 20	Reasonably aggressive	80% stocks 20% bonds
10 to 20	Less aggressive (unless you are behind schedule)	65% stocks 25% bonds 10% cash
Less than 10	Safe/conservative	40% stocks 40% bonds 20% cash

College

YEARS LEFT	INVESTMENT STYLE	ASSET ALLOCATION
More than 15	Aggressive	90% stocks 10% bonds
7 to 15	Reasonably aggressive	75% stocks 25% bonds
3 to 7	Less aggressive	65% stocks 35% bonds
Less than 3	Safe/protective	40% stocks 40% bonds 20% cash

Buying A Home

YEARS LEFT	INVESTMENT STYLE	ASSET ALLOCATION
5	Somewhat aggressive	65% stocks 35% bonds
3 to 5	Balanced	45% stocks 35% bonds 20% cash
Less than 3	Safe/protective	25% stocks 40% bonds 35% cash

cash. This, while not as well positioned to take advantage of market upturns, is better protected from dropping stock prices and is worth considering for an investor who may have a shorter term goal—say, buying a home in five to ten years—and still needs some measure of growth.

A conservative mix might comprise 40 to 50 percent stocks, 20 percent bonds, and upwards of 30 percent in cash. Following through on the time frame theme, this kind of allocation would be ideal for someone nearing retirement who doesn't want to risk any substantial drops in her portfolio.

For more sample allocations, have a look at the box above.

Diversification and asset allocation are two powerful investing strategies.

Be careful about being too conservative if you have a long investment time frame.

Portfolio

CNBC

Stocks: Your Share of the Pie

When it comes to the world of stock ownership, it pays to know your subject inside and out, taking in everything from what a stock actually is to what it represents to you as an investor.

Stock Basics

What Stocks Mean

Stocks are a form of equity investment, which means that when you buy stock in a company you actually own a small piece of that business. Companies usually issue stock to raise money. The overall number of shares that are sold to the investing public is called the float.

The reason for buying stock in a company is simple—you believe that the company is a worthy entity that will prosper and, in turn, increase the value of your stock holdings. There's a downside, of course—there's no guarantee that the company is going to do well, which could conceivably lessen the value of your stock investment.

But that inherent risk—and, as we'll see later, there are ways to reduce the risk of stock investing—is what makes stocks one of the best performing investments. Remember, since before the Great Depression, certain stocks have returned an average in excess of 12 percent a year.

Types of Stocks

By far the majority of stock that's bought and traded around the world is called **common stock**. This buys you a slice of the company, and you may also receive any dividends that the company generates, although there's no guarantee of that. If the

Over What Counter?

One term you'll hear is the over-the-counter market, or OTC. Tens of thousands of public companies are traded by phone and computer. While several thousand of them are included in the NASDAQ system, most aren't large enough to qualify for any sort of exchange. As a rule, these are the diciest of all stocks to invest in—they often have little in the way of profit or operating history, and tracking news about the company and its price can be difficult.

company goes under, common stock ownership also entitles you to a share of any assets that remain after other creditors have been paid off.

By contrast, **preferred stock** is more of a sure thing. Dividends are guaranteed and are often larger than those paid common stock shareholders. Additionally, should the company fold, preferred stock shareholders get their cut of remaining assets before common stock holders. On the downside, should the company blossom, preferred dividends don't increase accordingly.

Stock Exchanges

Stocks are bought and sold on three major exchanges in the United States. The biggest and best known is the **New York Stock Exchange**. With some 3,000 companies listed, the NYSE houses most of the behemoths of American capitalism, including a majority of the companies that comprise the Dow Jones Industrial Average—often seen as a Bellwether of the American economy. The **American Stock Exchange** comprises roughly 800 companies that, as a rule, are not large enough to get to the NYSE. The **NASDAQ National Market System** has more than 4,000 companies and is the busiest of the three exchanges in terms of the number of shares traded. The Nasdaq is also a purely electronic exchange—unlike the NYSE and American, there's no trading floor and all transactions take place electronically.

In addition to the big three, there are also several smaller, regional exchanges located in Boston, Chicago, and other cities.

Stock Glossary

Here's a sampling of other stock terms that will likely prove useful:

Capital Gains: This is the profit you realize after you sell a stock that's gone up in value. There are long-term capital gains for stocks you own for more than a year and short-term capital gains, which cover stocks held less than one year. Each type of capital gain is taxed differently.

Indexes: These, like the Dow Jones, are groupings of stocks whose composite price is tracked. Like the Dow, indexes are designed to offer a snapshot of how certain stocks—and the market as a whole—are performing. Some of the better known indexes are the Standard and Poor's 500 and the Wilshire 5,000.

Initial Public Offering (IPO): This is when a company offers stock for the first time. IPOs get a lot of publicity, particularly if a company's stock value soars in the first hours of trading. However, IPOs often fall as fast as they rise, making them a dicey investment choice. Moreover, it's often impossible for the general investing public to buy top-quality IPOs, as they usually go to institutional investors.

Penny Stocks: The cheapest of the cheap OTC stocks, so named because shares can be bought for mere pennies. These are often listed on what are called the Pink Sheets (it's printed on pink paper). Avoid penny stocks like your worst in-law, as the companies have, at best, highly suspect futures.

Proxy: Although most of the buzz about stocks concerns profit and loss, owning stock also means having a voice in how the company is run. Companies have annual meetings at which shareholders vote on significant company decisions. You don't have to attend to vote—instead, as a shareholder, you receive a proxy in the mail through which you can vote on naming a board of directors and other proposals that mandate shareholder approval.

Secondary Offering: This is a new issue of stock from a company that has already floated stock.

Spreads: Although a spread is employed with all stocks, it is most noticeable with OTC stocks. The spread represents the difference between the asking price—what you have to pay to buy the stock—and the bid price, which represents what you could get if you sold it right away. The Nasdaq has taken heat in recent years over allegations that the spreads of some of its stocks are unnecessarily large.

Stock Splits: Like the name suggests, a stock split represents a division of an existing stock. For instance, if a company declares a two-for-one split, the stock price is effectively divided in half and you, the investor, end up with twice as many shares. However, since the price per share is cut in half, your investment isn't worth any more, at least when the split takes effect.

▲ **Stocks represent one of the best long-term investments available.**

▼ **Penny stocks are among the riskiest stocks you can buy.**

Stock Types

There are many types of stocks, depending on how you want to break them down. They have various sizes and fulfill different needs for various investors. In this section, we'll take a look at some major types of stocks and what separates them, and begin to get a feel for how they may fit into different portfolios.

Major Stock Categories

Growth Stocks

WHAT THEY ARE: These companies are growing in both revenue and profit and, as such, offer that same sort of opportunity to investors willing to go along for the ride. Ideally, they'll increase both their revenue and profitability over a long period of time. Such companies tend to reinvest most of the money that they produce to fuel growth, so they generally don't pay any sort of dividend to investors.

WHAT THEY'RE NOT: These can be among the most aggressive of stocks to own. Investing in them is predicated on an optimistic, steady upturn in the company's fortunes, and any fall off from that trend— or, even worse, failure to realize any potential—can devastate the stock price. Small-growth stocks—also called emerging growth stocks— can be the riskiest, since they are often fighting for market share with larger, more established competitors. If, however, they can grab and build on a niche, they can also prove to be the most profitable.

Value Stocks

WHAT THEY ARE: Value stocks are similar to growth stocks—you hope both go up in value. The difference is a value stock offers more of a perceived discount—put another way, the price of the stock doesn't reflect the true value of the company. As we'll see later, that can be determined through a variety of calculations, including how much the company owns in terms of assets and how much it might be worth if it were broken up.

WHAT THEY'RE NOT: Not a sure bet. In many ways, you're trying to latch onto a stock whose price is out of kilter with the company's value. Should the company's performance not bear out higher values, the price can stay down.

Income Stocks

Remember the discussion on the effect of interest rates on stock prices? Income stocks are particularly touchy— when interest rates go down, income stocks tend to react positively, since their dividends become more competitive with bonds. But, the opposite is true if interest rates rise.

Income Stocks

WHAT THEY ARE: Not every stock is geared to providing their investors with a big payoff through growth. Some are great when it comes to producing a steady income. Income stocks are generally well-established, solid profit companies that consistently pay out high dividends. Income stocks include such entities as utilities, banks, and real estate-related stocks.

How Size Matters

Another consideration in choosing a stock is its size. That's known as market capitalization, or market cap, which represents the overall market value of a company's stock. There are three primary groups—small, medium, and large caps. Here's a breakdown of what they mean and other elements associated with the three classifications.

	Small Caps	Mid Caps	Large Caps
Size	Less than $1 billion market cap.	Between $1 billion and $7 billion market cap.	Greater than $7 billion market cap.
Characteristics	Small companies with significant growth potential.	Larger, more established than small caps, but many companies have significant growth potential.	Well-known, established companies, including so-called blue chip stocks.
Growth Patterns	Volatile. Can either blossom or bomb.	Varies. Some have room to grow, others have topped out.	Very controlled and limited. If any upside growth potential, will only happen very slowly.
Why Invest	Generally inexpensive; can pay off big if company flourishes.	Less volatile than small caps, with growth possibilities. Greater risk of stagnant growth.	Relatively safe. Good source of dividend income.

WHAT THEY'RE NOT: Don't look for much price appreciation with these.

Cyclical Stocks

WHAT THEY ARE: More so than other types of stocks, these are tied to economic cycles. For instance, large manufacturing companies tend to do well when good economic conditions create demand for their products. But they tend to suffer when the economy takes a downturn—even though their operating costs are the same, stock prices tend to go down since demand is also dropping.

WHAT THEY'RE NOT: These are not necessarily solid plays. Not only do you have to find a good company, you have to invest when the economy plays to its strength.

International Stocks

WHAT THEY ARE: These are stocks from overseas companies. They can range from exceedingly well-known companies to the most obscure, covering everything from established industrialized nations to relatively undeveloped countries. These can often effectively complement domestic stocks, as overseas stocks can often act as a buffer to downturns in U.S. markets. They can also provide significant growth opportunities.

WHAT THEY'RE NOT: On the downside, overseas companies can suffer downturns as readily as their American counterparts. And, as we noted earlier, in some parts of the world, there's the added concern of political instability.

▲ Match a stock to your goals—growth for long-term, income for cash flow.

▼ Don't ignore risk, particularly with smaller, less-established companies.

Things to Consider

Choosing Stocks: The Basics

There are many ways to evaluate a stock's profitability, but before we get into the specifics, it makes sense to tackle some global dos and don'ts about analyzing stocks.

Five Stocks Dos and Don'ts

Before breaking down a stock's numbers and other criteria, look at any stock you're considering with these five essential ideas in mind:

Know What the Company Does

This seems like a no-brainer, right? You'd be surprised how many investors drop good money on stocks that they don't really understand. But it pays to know precisely how a company earns its money—pick up an annual report and read about the company's operations. Not only will that give you an idea of how reliable its overall business operation might be—companies, after all, can make money in all sorts of creative, strange ways—but you may also find out that it trades in an industry or product with which you're familiar.

Check out:
▸ Company Operations
▸ Management
▸ Operating History
▸ Revenue Sources

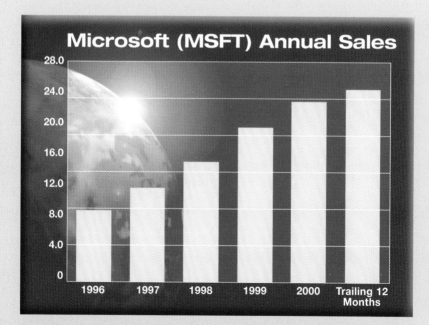

Microsoft (MSFT) Annual Sales

Steadily increasing sales are one good barometer of a company's growth and, hence, its stock performance. This shows Microsoft's sales since 1996.

Consider Several Basics When

Is the Company Headed in the Right Direction?

While you've got an annual report in your hands, check out how the company's sales are doing. Ideally, you're looking for that number to rise over time. Granted, this is more predictable with established companies than it is with a startup, but growing sales figures are a solid sign that things are on the right track.

Check out:
▸ Sales Trends
▸ Growth
▸ Profitability

Is the Company Competitive?

One general rule of thumb when analyzing any stock is to compare its overall performance with other similar companies. That makes for a useful apples-to-apples comparison. For instance, you may discover that a company with an attractively priced stock has a higher growth rate than other companies in its field. By the same token, you may also find that a company is lagging behind its competitors. As we'll see later, ratios are a great way of making these sorts of important comparisons.

Check out:
▸ Sales versus competitors
▸ Profits versus competitors
▸ Growth versus competitors

Look at the Company's Finances

A company may be selling its product faster than it can manufacture it, but if the debt incurred by those manufacturing costs outpaces sales, that company may be headed toward a cliff. That said, look at a company's overall financial health—debt, spending patterns, and the like—to get a feel for how well the company may be managed. We'll tackle this in greater detail in the next section covering the income statement and balance sheet.

Check out:
▸ Debt
▸ Assets
▸ Major Expenses

Don't Stop with the Annual Report

Although annual reports can be a great starting point for analyzing a stock, bear in mind that they represent a major public relations effort. Companies spend a lot of time and money to make the report as flattering as possible. Take what you read with a grain of salt and with the determination to include other information sources in your decision.

Check out:
▸ Ratios
▸ Analyst Reports
▸ Stock Price Movement

Finding Data

There are a variety of places where you can track down the stock data discussed here. Check out CNBC television, newspaper business sections, finance and investing magazines and a variety of other broadcast and published sources. Nor should you overlook Internet sites, such as Morningstar, CNBC.com and other web offerings.

▲ Look for companies with consistent sales growth.

▼ Watch out for excessive debt and other financial problems.

Inside the Financial Statement

A company's annual report isn't always the best place for investment information. Words and pretty pictures can be crafted to make things seem rosier than they are.

But inside the annual report is the company's income statement and balance sheet—a comprehensive itemization of the company's financial activities. Looking through these statements—and understanding them—can often reveal a great deal about a company's prospects.

Breaking Down an Income Statement and Balance Sheet

The following is a breakdown of some of the major terms you'll find on an income statement and balance sheet, along with some ideas of what to look for:

Cash and Securities. This refers to money the company has on hand, in the form of both cash and liquid securities. It's a good idea to compare cash and securities and the amount of current liability— if the liability is larger than a company's cash and securities, the company may struggle to pay its short-term bills.

Receivables. This is what customers owe the company. Compare this figure with overall sales; if receivables are lagging, that may mean the company's having a hard time collecting what it's owed.

Allowances. This relatively small figure stands for things such as product returns, refunds, discounts, and other similar deductions from sales. Look at it over several years' time. If it is increasing, that may

suggest growing dissatisfaction with the company's products.

Current Assets. The sum of the company's current assets, meaning any funds that can be turned into cash in one year or less. Compare this with current liabilities to make sure the company has enough funds on hand to meet its short-term debt.

Property and Equipment. This represents the company's "non-current" assets, including such things as physical plants, machinery, office equipment, and vehicles. This, too, should be compared with sales figures, as it may raise concerns about overly aggressive expansion, such as construction of new facilities that can't be justified by growth in sales.

Current Liabilities. This is the debt that the company is due to pay within the next year. Again, compare this with sales and assets to make sure that debt isn't outpacing what the company is taking in.

Total Liabilities and Equity. The sum of all that the company owes along with the amount of common stock owned—put another way, all that is effectively owned by somebody else. This figure must be the same as the number of total assets, since everything in the company has to be owned by someone.

Total Revenues. Total amount of sales before taxes are deducted. While a big jump may seem dandy, it's essential to compare it with other items, such as earnings per share.

Cost of Sales. These are charges the company accrued as a direct result of sales. If this number is larger than revenues, duck—it's a sign that growth in sales is coming at far too expensive a price.

Other Expenses. These detail other costs that are not directly connected to sales, such as administrative costs, research and development, and other similar costs. Again, compare this number with sales and other income to make sure it's not too high compared with what the company is taking in.

Pre-Tax Income. The amount of income or loss the company had before taxes. This can be a handy number to watch for, as it can reveal a company that turns a profit, only to pay out more in taxes.

Income Tax. While most of us are tickled to death to get a tax refund, such is not necessarily the case with a large company. Some com-panies lose so much money that they actually have tax money returned to them—that's never a positive sign.

Net Income. Income after taxes. A telling bottom line, as it represents the most accurate figure of a company's actual income.

EPS Primary. This represents the earnings per individual share of stock and offers a further breakdown of whether a company is making or losing money.

EPS Diluted. This is earnings per share that takes into account additional items, such as outstanding purchase options and other factors that can increase the overall number of shares. In many cases, this can further reduce earnings per share, since more shares divvying up earnings means lower earnings per share.

Check All the Pieces

One of the keys to understanding and using a balance sheet and income statement is to incorporate as much of the available information as possible to get a complete picture of a stock. As we mentioned above, a company that seems to be blowing the roof off on sales may seem great, but prohibitive cost of sales can deflate that somewhat. The more you can piece together, the more you'll ultimately know about a stock's past and its prospects.

Look for positive signs such as growing revenues and profit.

Watch out for excessive debt and liabilities.

More Ways to Evaluate Stocks

A company's numbers aren't the only way to scour for winning stocks. Here, we look at some additional techniques that can prove handy in assessing a stock's prospects.

Four Useful Ratios

Whether in the newspaper, an online chat group or on CNBC's *Market Watch*, you'll hear a lot of terminology concerning various ratios and how they apply to stocks. Here's a breakdown of four of them:

Price-Earnings Ratio (P/E)

WHAT IT IS: This is a basic ratio that values stocks by showing how much investors will spend for $1 of earnings. It divides the price of the stock by earnings per share.

Example: A $20 stock that earned $1 per share during one year has a P/E of 20.

WHAT IT MEANS: An important indicator, this gives an idea of how expensive a stock price really is in relation to what the company is actually earning.

WHAT TO LOOK FOR: Several things. First, the higher the P/E, the greater the risk, since the stock's price is more out of line with what the company is making. But a high P/E also means that investors are expecting big things from the company in the future and are willing to pay for it.

HOW TO USE IT: Compare a company's P/E with competitors and within its industry. Look at the company's growth rate versus its P/E. A low P/E with a high annual growth rate may mean a great stock.

Wrinkles: Trailing Earnings P/E compares price with past earnings. Projected Earnings P/E compares price with expected earnings. Use both to get a feel for where a company has been and where it may be headed.

Price/Book Ratio (P/B)

WHAT IT IS: This measures stock price against a company's net worth (also known as book value). It is calculated by dividing the current stock price by a company's book value.

Example: A stock selling for $30 a share with a book value of $10 a share has a P/B of three.

WHAT IT MEANS: Some think the P/B is more useful than the P/E, because it's based on what a company is truly worth rather than what it earns.

WHAT TO LOOK FOR: The lower the P/B, the greater the possibility that the stock is a bargain, since investors aren't paying a premium yet.

HOW TO USE IT: While the P/B is a good barometer of a company's value, use this in context. A manufacturing stock with a lot of equipment will have a low P/B, while a software developer's value may be more in its ideas than its tangibles.

Price/Sales Ratio (P/S)

WHAT IT IS: Stock price measured against a company's sales. It's calculated by dividing a stock's current price by its revenue per share.

Example: A stock selling for $20 a share with revenue per share-sales of $15 has a P/S of 1.3.

WHAT IT MEANS: This is another useful tool, since sales figures—like the value of a company—are hard to tinker with.

WHAT TO LOOK FOR: The lower the P/S, the greater the chance that the stock price will rise. A P/S can also be used to examine companies which have yet to report any earnings, which makes a price-earnings ratio useless.

HOW TO USE IT: Since industries vary so much in profit margins, P/S is best used within the same industry for a fair comparison.

Dividend Yield

WHAT IT IS: This compares the dividend payout to shareholders versus the price of the stock. It's obtained by dividing the dividend by the per share price.

Example: A $60 stock paying $2 per share in dividends has a dividend yield of approximately 3.3 percent.

WHAT IT MEANS: Another measure of worth, since a healthy company often pays out solid dividends.

WHAT TO LOOK FOR: Some investors think that a high yield indicates that a stock is undervalued. By contrast, the lower the yield, the more an investor pays for the dividend the stock produces.

HOW TO USE IT: Dividend yield doesn't really apply to many growth companies which, while growing and healthy, reinvest dividends rather than pay them to shareholders.

Want to see how these various factors can come together? CNBC on MSN Money's stock screens let you search for stocks based on all sorts of criterion. The screen below reflects a search asking for high dividend yields and low price/earnings ratios:

CNBC

Symbol	Company Name	Debt to Equity Ratio	Current Dividend Yield	P/E Ratio: Current
AMCT	AMRESCO Capital Trust	0.00	797.00	2.30
BSRTS	Banyan Strategic Realty Trust	1.96	566.70	6.40
PHR	Philips International Realty Corp.	0.00	500.00	0.50
ASIPY	Anangel-American Shipholdings Limited	0.77	147.80	1.40
SID	Companhia Siderúrgica Nacional	0.64	135.30	1.40
MOYC	Moyco Technologies, Inc.	0.17	134.30	0.90
CLR	Clarion Commercial Holdings, Inc.	0.00	110.00	8.00
NCN	Nce Petrofund TR UTS WO PARVAL	0.54	53.70	3.00
RC	Grupo Radio Centro, S.A. de C.V.	0.23	46.20	3.90
AIK	Amer Ins Mtge Inv Ser 88	0.00	44.60	11.10
HUMP	Humphrey Hospitality Trust, Inc.	2.69	43.90	4.40
ELBT	Elbit Ltd.	0.00	39.00	5.60
AIP	American Israeli Paper Mills Limited	0.15	36.70	11.30
AIJ	Amer Ins Mtge Inv Ser 86	0.00	29.50	4.60
TRU	Torch Energy Royalty Trust	0.00	28.70	3.50
NAT	Nordic American Tanker Shipping Ltd.	0.25	28.60	4.30

▲ Ratios can be effective in evaluating stock performance.

▼ Use ratios in context—compare similar companies in similar industries.

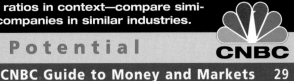

Other Stock Analyses

Now that your head is probably ready to implode from all the numbers that can be involved in selecting winning stocks, know that there are other ways of getting the job done. Again, though, it's important to get a feel for how they work and what their varied drawbacks and limitations might be.

Technical Analysis, Screens, Analysts Reports

Technical Analysis

Much of what we've covered until now has had to do with looking at a company's numbers, value, and products. This system is known as fundamental analysis. By contrast, some investors and analysts prefer to pay attention to a stock's trading activity as an indicator of whether it's a good play or not, often using charts to track trading patterns. This is called technical analysis.

Technical analysis largely breaks down into two components—price and volume. With price, analysts look for things such as the historical movement of the stock in order to establish benchmarks, such as a support level (the stock's established lowest price) and resistance level (conversely, the price that marks the top end of the price spectrum). It's a sign of bad things to come should a stock drop past its established support level (that can happen when particularly bad news comes out about a stock). By contrast, a stock that pushes past its resistance level may be set to take off even further. Technical advocates also look at volume (the amount of stock that's being traded) as an indicator of investor interest in the stock.

Bear in mind that many investors use technical and fundamental analysis in choosing stocks. It combines an examination of the company with the movement and characteristics of the company's stock.

Advantages

▶ **No Company Knowledge Needed.** Just watch price movement and activity.

▶ **Broader Knowledge.** Even if you pay attention to fundamentals, it doesn't hurt to know a stock's historical patterns.

▶ **Short-Term Usefulness.** Active traders often use technical analysis because, over the short term, a stock's price changes but its fundamentals don't.

"Systems"

There are scads of other ways to predict stock movement, ranging from the mundane to the insane. For instance, a number of years ago there was a newsletter that purported to predict stock activity based on the tides and solar and lunar phases. As a rule, skirt any "system" that trumpets any sort of stock selection grandeur. It's usually pure delusion.

Screens and Analysts Can Remove Much

Drawbacks

▸ **Earnings Matter.** Fundamental advocates argue that earnings drive price movement, not a stock's chart.

▸ **The Biggies.** If it means anything, investing giants like Peter Lynch and Warren Buffett stick with fundamentals.

Stock Screens

Thanks to the Internet, stock screens are now available to anyone with a computer and a modem. Screens take much of the legwork out of stock selection. With various types of wrinkles, they all pretty much operate in the same fashion—they let you specify the kind of stock you're looking for and, based on the information you provide, serve up the stocks that fit.

For instance, CNBC on MSN Money's Stock Screener (located at www.cnbc.com) lets you enter a number of parameters, including type of stock, momentum, and other information. Once you're done, the system kicks back stocks that match your guidelines.

Advantages

▸ **Automation.** Investors don't have to wade through numbers by themselves.

▸ **Speed.** Again, no getting bogged down with a ton of numbers.

▸ **Objectivity.** No sales pitch here, just straight feedback.

▸ **Customization.** Good screens let investors insert different criteria as they wish.

Drawbacks

▸ **Interpretation.** If you don't know what the various numbers and terms mean, it is hard to understand the results.

▸ **Cost.** Most screens are free—some are not. Unless they offer a specific function you can't live without, avoid those that charge.

Analysts

This option, like a stock screen, can also remove much of the individual effort involved in weeding through stocks. In this case, though, it's a human being rather than a software program. Analysts track stocks in great detail, watching price movement, earnings, news about the company, and any other factor. On top of that, analysts usually transfer that information into recommendations, suggesting when a stock should be bought, held, or sold.

Advantages

▸ **Convenience.** They do all the work, not you.

▸ **Comprehensive Research.** Analysts are often authorities in their particular field and are highly paid to break down a stock exhaustively.

▸ **Information.** Given their position, analysts often have access to data and insight unavailable to average investors.

Drawbacks

▸ **Cost.** Many places will charge you for access to analysts' reports.

▸ **Accuracy.** Analysts have been wrong more than once about where a stock is headed.

▸ **Involvement.** Listening to someone else is fine, but there's a lot to be said for doing your own legwork. You may have a better sense of your goals and how you intend to achieve them.

Consider every source of information you can when checking out a stock.

Watch out for unnecessary costs in accessing information and analysis.

of Investing's Legwork

Special Strategies

For most investors, the idea behind stocks is simple—research, buy and hope the company does well. But there are also some specific strategies that can be employed in stock investment. Some let you invest in different ways while others deal with elements of the investment process itself.

Four Variations

Short Selling

Here, ironically enough, you "buy" a stock in the hope that the price will go down.

HOW IT WORKS: First, you need a margin account (see below). Then, you borrow shares of stock from other accounts and sell them. If the price drops, you buy the shares again at the lower price, return them, and pocket the difference.

WHEN YOU WOULD DO THIS: When the market as a whole is dropping, in the hope of taking advantage of declining prices.

Short Funds

Believe it or not, there are mutual funds whose primary activity is shorting stocks. These, which often have the word "bear" stuck into their names, are purportedly designed to take advantage of dropping market conditions (hence "bear," referring to bear markets). They may work in the short run but, overall, their records are poor, since the overall trend of the market has always been up (see accompanying chart as an example).

WHAT CAN GO WRONG: If the stock jumps in price, the short seller has to make up the difference—for instance, if you short a $10 stock and the price goes to $20, you lose $10 for every share you shorted.

BOTTOM LINE: While investors may be tempted to try to turn a profit when things are going badly, short selling is a dicey investment strategy. It's better and far more reliable to try to pick winners, not losers.

Buying on Margin

With margin, you're investing borrowed money.

HOW IT WORKS: First, you set up a margin account with a brokerage house. You put up collateral—usually stocks or cash—and the broker lends you up to half their value (and charges you interest on the loan). You then use these funds to buy stock.

WHEN YOU WOULD DO THIS: If the market's on the way up and you want to take full advantage, buying on margin lets you invest more than the cash you may actually have on hand. If things go well, you pay off the loan and have profit left over.

WHAT CAN GO WRONG: Lots. For one thing, the stock you buy on margin may just sit there or drop—at worst, you may be stuck with both a loser and a loan to repay. Even worse is a **margin call**. This happens when the market drops quickly, cutting the stock's value in half. You have to maintain at least a 50 percent equity in your investment or you may get a margin call from your broker. A margin call requires you to put up more collateral to cover your loan—if you can't, the stock is immediately sold, and you lose your entire investment.

BOTTOM LINE: Really dicey way to play. Best avoided.

Limit Order

Limit orders let you specify buy and sell prices.

HOW IT WORKS: You instruct a broker to buy or sell a stock at a certain price or better.

WHEN YOU WOULD DO THIS: Ideal if you expect a stock's price to change. For instance, if a stock is at $35 and you want to buy it at $30, the order is carried out if the stock drops to that level. If by chance the stock goes even lower, the broker executes the buy at the lower price. By contrast, if you put in an order to sell the same stock at $40 and the stock jumps to $45, you get the higher sale price.

WHAT CAN GO WRONG: The biggest problem occurs when a stock simply doesn't move as much as you think. For instance, a buy at $30 for a great stock that only dips to $31 can cut you out of a wonderful investment because of a single dollar difference in price.

BOTTOM LINE: Sensible strategy that helps hedge your bets.

Stop Loss Order

This is a way to protect your profit or limit your losses.

HOW IT WORKS: Tell your broker to sell a stock when it reaches a particular price. For example, if

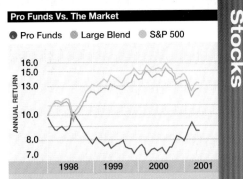

Pro Funds Vs. The Market

● Pro Funds ● Large Blend ○ S&P 500

To illustrate how difficult it can be to be successful at selling short, have a look at the performance of a bear fund, The ProFunds Bear Fund Investor Shares. As you can see, it moves in the opposite direction to the Standard and Poor's 500 Index and other similar mutual funds that try to pick winning stocks rather than shorting them. It performed reasonably well in late 2000 and early 2001—when the market as a whole was falling—but, over the long term, its overall trend has been down.

you bought a stock at $20, it flies to $50 and you institute a stop loss order at $40, at the very least you'll make a $20 per share profit.

WHEN YOU WOULD DO THIS: As the above example shows, this is a smart way to protect your profit. It can also protect you from getting killed by a plummeting stock. For instance, if you buy a stock at $30, put in a stop loss order for $25 and the stock careens down to $10, you've just saved yourself $15 per share.

WHAT CAN GO WRONG: Don't set a stop loss order too close to a stock's current price—that can leave you too little room to recover from what may well be a temporary drop in value. As a rule, experts suggest a stop loss of 20 percent below a stock's current level.

BOTTOM LINE: Again, a sensible strategy that, if employed intelligently, can save you money.

Stop loss and limit orders can be effective at locking in profits and limiting losses.

Selling short and buying on margin are risky ways to invest.

How to Buy Stock

Feel that you know enough now to start picking winning stocks? There's one last step in the formula. As opposed to days gone by when using the traditional brokerage house was pretty much the only way to purchase stocks, there are several options available to investors today. Like so much to do with investing, there are advantages and drawbacks to each.

Ways to Get in the Game

Here's a rundown of the various ways you can buy stock.

Traditional Brokerage House

This is the most established method of buying stock. You open an account at a brokerage house, and you're usually assigned a broker or account executive who works with you to develop an investment plan and select appropriate investments. Large brokerage houses also have a research department to provide high quality information to clients.

On the upside:

▸ **Guidance.** The traditional broker-client relationship establishes a personal, one-on-one approach to investing. Brokers work to understand your financial goals and make recommendations accordingly.

▸ **Experience.** Traditional brokerage houses have been through up and down markets. This experience is invaluable in turbulent market environments.

On the downside:

▸ **Expense.** Under most broker-client agreements, you pay a commission every time you buy or sell. Depending on the brokerage house, that can be very expensive.

▸ **Objectivity.** Some would argue that, since the broker only gets paid when you buy or sell, his or her recommendations may not always be purely in your best interests.

Shopping Tip: If you're interested in a full-service broker, be sure to ask about any variations on the broker-client arrangement. Some full-service houses have developed different programs, such as a flat annual fee that still lets you work with a stockbroker.

Discount Brokerage House

Discount houses offer a cost-effective alternative to pricey full-service houses. Here, the commission you pay when you buy or sell a stock is cut drastically, often to just a few dollars a trade.

Risk-Free Trial

If you're new to investing and want to check out your skills without actually risking money, many online brokers and other sites offer stock-picking games. You do everything you would normally do when investing—research, buying, and tracking your choices—only you don't risk any money.

On the upside: This is a whole lot less expensive than conventional full-service brokers. Additionally, the broker usually gives investors access to research reports and other tools and information with which to make investment decisions.

On the downside: Since you're paying dirt-cheap commissions, you don't work with a broker on a one-on-one basis.

Shopping Tip: Be sure to ask the brokerage house about access to research and analysis. Some houses offer everything to everybody, while others make investors pay extra for certain types of services and investment research.

Online Brokerage Houses

Both full-service and discount houses have brought their operations onto the World Wide Web, offering trading capabilities, research, and other investment services.

On the upside: If you're comfortable with a computer and modem, online brokerage services are a boon to investors. You can place trades quickly and efficiently, carry out research, track your investments, and perform an array of other jobs, all in a fraction of the time that it used to take and at a fraction of the cost of traditional brokerage services.

On the downside: For one thing, online brokerages suffer technical breakdowns and gluts in the system that can slow service.

Shopping Tip: If you're interested in an online broker, try calling its customer service line or logging onto their site in the middle of a busy trading day. That can give you an idea of how reliable the service might be.

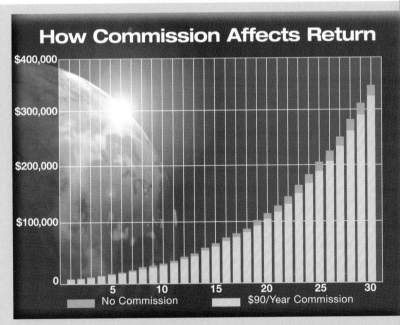

How Commission Affects Return

No Commission $90/Year Commission

It may seem incidental, but it pays to be aware of the expense of investing. To illustrate this, have a look at the effects of a seemingly paltry $90 annual commission on a 30-year investment. By taking what seems to be next to nothing out of the amount you invest each year, you lose more than $16,000 if you average a 10 percent annual return.

▲ Want a personal investing relationship? Look to full-service brokers.

▼ Full-service brokers can be much more expensive than discount brokers.

Costs and Services

CNBC

Other Ways to Buy Stock

Buying stock isn't limited to calling your broker or going online and placing an order. There are other avenues to obtaining quality stock, not to mention other strategies to amassing a stock portfolio in a systematic, intelligent manner.

DPPs, DRIPs, and Other Ways to Build Your Holdings

Direct Purchase Plans (DPPs)

WHAT THEY ARE: Direct Purchase Plans allow you to buy stock directly from the company that issues the stock.

WHY THAT'S GOOD: Unlike conventional stock purchases, DPPs don't levy any sort of sales commission. Estimates are that more than 2,000 public companies offer some sort of direct purchase program to investors.

WHAT TO BEAR IN MIND: Although DPPs don't have sales commissions, some companies do charge what they call "administrative fees." Also, don't buy a stock because it's free of sales charges—do the same investigative legwork you would with any stock to make sure it's a good investment.

HOW TO FIND OUT MORE: Contact a company's corporate offices—or visit their website—to find out if they offer a Direct Purchase Plan.

Dividend Reinvestment Plans (DRIPs)

WHAT THEY ARE: Once you own a stock, these let you set up a program that automatically reinvests any dividends you receive in additional stock.

WHY THAT'S GOOD: It's a great way to build your holdings automatically. Most DRIP plans have no sales charge. Some even discount the price of shares bought via DRIPs.

WHAT TO BEAR IN MIND: Again, a DRIP does not necessarily a good investment make. Be sure to check out the stock thoroughly.

HOW TO FIND OUT MORE: Call any company you're interested in—or check out their website—for further details on DRIP availability.

Dollar-Cost Averaging

WHAT IT IS: A plan in which you invest a fixed amount of money on a regular basis—for instance, $200

Automated Success

The more you can automate your investment program, either through programs such as DRIPs or an averaging strategy, the better your chances for long-term success. Not only can they put your investing on a form of autopilot, they are effective ways to build your holdings and reduce risk.

Check to See If You Can Buy Stock Straight

every month, no matter what the stock price happens to be doing.

WHY THAT'S GOOD: It's an automatic way to build holdings in a systematic manner. And, if the price of the stock goes down, it lets you accumulate more shares faster, since you're buying more at a lower price per share.

WHAT TO BEAR IN MIND: Again, make sure you have confidence in the stock you're dollar-cost averaging into, as it's hard to mitigate a stock that's gone down in value and languishes there.

Value Averaging

WHAT IT IS: A variation on dollar-cost averaging. Instead of investing the same amount of money every time, each investment is adjusted to a prearranged schedule.

Example: You want to invest $200 every month. At the end of the first month, your stock has gone down in value to $190. You would then invest $210 to bring the overall two-month value up to $400. On the other hand, if the stock had risen in value to $220, you would only have to invest $180.

WHY THAT'S GOOD: Like dollar-cost averaging, value averaging is a systematic way to build holdings.

WHAT TO BEAR IN MIND: Some studies suggest value averaging is more effective than dollar-cost averaging, since you're able to accumulate more shares at a lower cost per share.

Lump Sum

Month 1	Invest $10,000 at $100 per share	Value	$10,000
Month 2	Stock drops to $75 a share	Value	$7,500
Month 3	Stock at $90 a share	Value	$9,000
Month 4	Stock at $100 a share	Value	$10,000
Month 5	Stock at $110 a share	Value	$11,000

Dollar-Cost Averaging

Month 1	Invest $2,000 at $100 a share	Value	$2,000
Month 2	Invest $2,000 at $75 a share	Overall value	$3,500
Month 3	Invest $2,000 at $90 a share	Overall value	$6,200
Month 4	Invest $2,000 at $100 a share	Overall value	$8,889
Month 5	Invest $2,000 at $110 a share	Overall value	$11,777

This data illustrates how dollar-cost averaging can often prove more effective than simply investing a lump sum. Under this scenario, a $10,000 lump sum investment grows to $11,000 in five months. However, by investing $2,000 each month for five months, a dollar-cost averaging program allows for more shares at a lower price, resulting in an overall value of $11,777 after the same five-month period.

Look to automatic investment programs and strategies to build wealth.

Don't invest in a stock just because they offer DPPs or DRIPS.

from the Company

CNBC

More Ways to Buy— Initial Public Offerings

Another popular—yet volatile—way to invest in stocks is through initial public offerings (IPOs). Here's a rundown of how they work and how investors can approach them intelligently.

Inside Initial Public Offerings

Many have heard of investors who made millions in a few hours or days through initial public offerings. Some of these anecdotes are true, but for each of these stories there are many crash-and-burn disasters.

How They Work

An initial public offering takes place when a company sells its stock to the general public for the first time—usually to fund plans for expanding the business.

▶ **The First Steps.** First, an investment bank agrees to underwrite the company wishing to go public—that means it agrees to buy all available stock and subsequently resell it. The bank then sets a price that they believe fairly represents the value of the company—taking into account current market conditions and expectations.

▶ **First Jolt of Reality.** Remember that the investment bank just wants to sell the stock and is less interested in its price movement after trading begins. In the end, that means large institutional buyers usually get the fairest prices available on an IPO.

▶ **Second Jolt of Reality.** Since institutional investors have the money, not only do they get the best prices, they usually are able to grab onto the best, most attractive IPOs.

What About Individual Investors?

Since it seems as though institutional investors pretty much corner the attractive IPO market, it behooves individual investors to be careful when considering IPOs.

▶ **Availability.** While it may seem otherwise, the IPO market isn't as one-sided as it might appear to be. Many brokers now say they have a variety of initial public offerings available to clients.

Secondary Issues

A variation on the IPO theme is what is known as a secondary offering. This happens when a company, having already issued its first wave of stock, decides it wants to raise even more capital through another sale of stock to the public.

▶ **Third Jolt of Reality.** Unfortunately, again, IPOs aren't as accessible as many investors might like. Although brokers now claim greater access for individual clients, many require significant account minimums—$100,000 and even higher—to take part in any sale of initial public offerings. That policy is likely due to the speculative nature of IPOs—those with the most money, so the reasoning probably goes, can best take the hit if an IPO falls off the cliff.

Still Hungry for IPOs?

If you qualify—or are looking for other ways to access the IPO market—bear these suggestions in mind.

▶ **Read the Prospectus.** Like any stock, an IPO has to publish a legal prospectus outlining the specifics of the stock. In this case, it's a preliminary prospectus.

▶ **Watch for Rapid Price Movement.** If you're able to buy into an IPO from the start—or are trying to pick up shares on the first day or so of trading—keep an eye peeled for volatile price movements. Even IPOs which fly right out of the gate often see their prices fall within the first few days—or hours—of trading.

▶ **Give It Some Time.** If an IPO interests you, try watching and waiting. Again, if the price of the stock falls within the first several days, that means more shares for you at attractive prices.

▶ **Do Your Homework.** Regardless of the hysteria surrounding certain IPOs, the underlying companies still need to know what they're doing if the stocks are to prove a good investment. Be sure to research an IPO as you would any other stock.

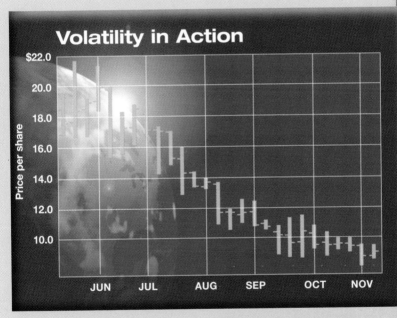

Volatility in Action

To show how volatile IPOs can be when they first start trading, have a look at a long-range chart of Instinet Group. When the stock went public in May 2000, note the wide swings in price during the first few weeks of trading (not to mention the heavy trading volume). Note, too, that the longer the stock is in play, the more narrow the trading range and the lower the volume as the buzz over an IPO slowly fizzles out.

IPOs have gotten the reputation as a great spot to make money—fast.

More often than not, IPOs sold to individual investors aren't worth the time.

Still Get the Hottest IPOs

CNBC

Trading by Insiders

While insider trading may conjure up images of unscrupulousness—Gordon Gekko in the movie *Wall Street* cajoling an innocent young broker into supplying him with inside dope—insider trading is, in fact, something that's common and, for the most part, above-board. Moreover, it can prove helpful to many investors.

The Workings of Trading by Insiders

What It Is

A company "insider" may be an executive or a member of the board of directors of a publicly traded company. Given their position, they're naturally privy to a good deal of detailed information that can affect the fortunes of the stock. When they buy or sell blocs of shares in the company, it's known as insider activity.

Insider Data

If insider trading interests you, know that there are any number of Web-based sources of information and analysis. One is MoneyCentral.com (see accompanying chart), which offers current information on insider buying and selling activity. Other sites and publications attempt to further quantify insider activity, building statistical-based indices to try to establish firm correlations between insider activity and subsequent stock price movement.

What Else Is Involved

The Securities and Exchange Commission closely regulates insider activity. It requires insiders to make public any time they engage in buying or selling company stock, including stock options.

How That Can Work for Other investors

The rationale is rather simple. Some investors follow insider activity in hopes of gaining insight into a particular stock. The thinking goes that an insider buying stock in the company is optimistic about where the stock may be headed; by contrast, an insider dumping stock may be worried about the company's prospects. After all, by virtue of their proximity to the company, insiders are assumed to have the inside track as to what's going right—or what's going wrong.

Is It Legal?

Yes. It's perfectly OK for insiders to buy and sell stock. But it is illegal for them to use their "inside" knowledge to manipulate the market.

Does Tracking Insider Trading Actually Work?

To a certain extent, it apparently does. Recent studies have found that, on many occasions, insider buying activity occurred when the going value of a stock was, in fact, depressed when compared with its actual value. Insiders often buy stock at low price-earnings ratios or when prices are depressed compared to a stock's book value. Studies have cited the following factors as examples of information that may influence insider activity:

▸ Knowledge of upcoming price increases for products, marketing campaigns, new product lines, and other elements that can impact productivity and profitability.

▸ Knowledge of company restructuring, such as the pending sale of an unprofitable operation or discontinuation of an unprofitable product or service.

▸ Knowledge of other pending company activity or news, including an expected influx of capital or the elimination of some form of significant debt.

By the same token, studies have indicated that insiders often sell significant blocs of stocks when a company's prospects appear headed for a downturn. Factors in this

can include unexpected increases in debt load, poor sales performance of a highly touted product and other sorts of news or developments that can depress a company's stock.

Is the System Flawless?

Like any other sort of investment analysis, the answer is no, insider activity isn't 100 percent reliable as a barometer of stock price movement. Although research has indicated that, in many cases, insider buying and selling may serve as reliable harbingers of upcoming movement in the price of a stock, it's by no means cast in stone. For instance, company insiders—like any other investor—can sell stock for all sorts of reasons: they want to lock in a profit, limit losses, or they merely need the cash.

Watch the Insiders

CNBC.com offers information on a stock's recent insider buying and selling activity. To illustrate, here's a section from the insider report on Dell Computers:

Dell Computer Corporation: Insider Trading

The following is a summary view of the 20 most recent SEC Form 4 filings indicating completed transactions by corporate insiders or major shareholders. Click on a filer's name to see details of the transactions listed on the document. To view all transactions for the last 12 months, click All Transactions.

For a list of proposed transactions, see the Planned Sales tab.

Date	Name	Transaction	Num Shares	Price(s)	Value
10/04/01	TOPFER MORTON L	Sold	300,000	$22.74	$7 Mil
09/27/01	DELL MICHAEL S*	Purchased	4 Mil	$16.26 - 17.43	$72 Mil
09/10/01	LUCE THOMAS W III	Sold	25,000	$22.61	$565,250
07/05/01	JORDAN MICHAEL H	Sold	130,000	$26.00 - 27.00	$3 Mil
07/05/01	MARENGI JOSEPH A	Sold	448,571	$27.00	$12 Mil
07/05/01	SCHNEIDER JAMES M	Sold	100,000	$27.00	$3 Mil
07/03/01	PARRA ROSENDO G*	Sold	54,900	$26.27 - 26.78	$1 Mil
07/03/01	PARRA ROSENDO G	Sold	2,400	$26.55	$63,720
07/02/01	LUFT KLAUS S	Sold	115,200	$26.95 - 26.97	$3 Mil
06/29/01	JORDAN MICHAEL H	Sold	45,000	$26.00 - 27.50	$1 Mil
06/29/01	ROLLINS KEVIN B	Sold	845,000	$24.00 - 27.16	$21 Mil

* This filing is an amendment to a previous filing.

Insider filings are updated every Friday evening on Investor and are based on forms filed monthly with the SEC.

From this chart, you can see when the buy or sale took place, the person involved in the transaction (click on the person's name for more detailed information regarding insider trading history), the number of shares involved and the price of the buy or sale.

Insider trading can often be effective in forecasting a stock's movement.

Insider trading can happen for all sorts of reasons.

Company's Inner Circle

Bond Basics

If you think back to earlier parts of this book that discussed diversification and ways to spread your money around intelligently, you'll no doubt remember that bonds were a part of most equations. It's time to discuss this element of investing, one that can prove significant to a broad number of investors.

You Give, and You Receive

What Bonds Mean

Bonds are something of an inverse investment when compared with stocks. With a stock, you gain ownership in a company. By contrast, a bond is a loan that comes with a promise to pay back what the investor put up, plus interest, usually twice a year.

Types of Bonds

▶ **Corporate Bonds.** These are sold by companies to cover the expense of various activities, including corporate expansion and funding of everyday business activities.

Tax-Free or Not?

One problem some investors have with bonds is trying to decide between taxable and tax-free bonds. To do that, use a simple formula. Take the yield of a tax-free bond and divide it by one minus your tax bracket. For instance, a municipal bond yielding 5 percent bought by someone in the 28 percent tax bracket would have the taxable equivalent of 6.9 percent (5 divided by .72). That gives a simple answer—if you can find a bond (or any other taxed investment) whose yield is better than 6.9 percent, go for it. You come out ahead, even with the tax bite.

▶ **Treasury Bonds.** These come from the federal government and its agencies and comprise Treasury bills and Treasury notes. The government has recently ended its auctions of 30-year Treasury bonds.

▶ **Municipal Bonds.** Issued by state and local governments, these pick up the tab for various community projects, such as bridge and road building.

Bond Features

▶ **Interest Payback.** Bonds generally pay interest to investors according to a specified payback schedule. Each payment amount is also usually prearranged.

▶ **Return of Investment.** Bonds usually have a specified lifetime, also known as the "term." Once a bond reaches its term, investors get their investment back (also known as the principal).

What Makes Bonds Different

Like stocks, different kinds of bonds have advantages and drawbacks:

▶ **Corporate Bonds** generally pay investors the highest return (also called a yield). On the downside, that income is fully taxable. While bonds of top-rated companies are almost free of default risk, others may not be.

▶ **Treasury Bonds** don't offer the returns that some corporate bonds do. But they are free of state and local taxes, which boosts their overall return a little.

▶ **Municipal Bonds** have the best tax situation you can find—they are free of federal taxes and may be free of state and local taxes if the buyer lives in the area where they're issued. However, since tax isn't eating into your returns, bear in mind that munis also offer lower rates of return than corporate bonds.

Check Out the Life of a Bond

Pay close attention to a bond's term. A bond is said to have matured if you hold it for the entire term, at which point you get back your principal. In general, bonds fall into three categories:

▶ **Short-term.** Anything less than three years.

▶ **Intermediate.** Five to 12 years.

▶ **Long-term.** These mature in 12 years or more.

The Term of the Bond Carries Several Implications:

▶ **Payout.** The longer the term, the higher the yield.

▶ **Payback.** The longer the bond, the longer you have to wait for maturity to get your principal back.

▶ **Interest Rate Risk.** The longer the term, the greater the risk that your bond's value will be affected by interest rate movement if you wish to sell it before maturity.

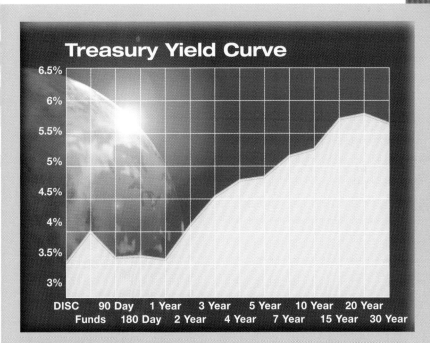

Treasury Yield Curve

| | DISC Funds | 90 Day 180 Day | 1 Year 2 Year | 3 Year 4 Year | 5 Year 7 Year | 10 Year 15 Year | 20 Year 30 Year |

As we mentioned above, how much a bond pays out in yield is determined, in large part, by the term of the bond. That results in a phenomenon known as the yield curve (pictured). This shows that, as a rule, the longer the term, the better the yield, although the specifics of the yield curve are changing all the time.

▲ Consider risk and payout when looking into bonds.

▼ Don't automatically assume that tax-free is a better investment.

Breaking Down Bonds

Now that we've gotten our feet wet, bond-wise, we can proceed to take a closer look at the various types of bonds. Given that they all have different characteristics and features, they also have their own pluses and drawbacks.

Corporate, Treasury and Municipal Bonds—A Closer View

Corporate Bonds

As discussed earlier, corporate bonds come from firms that are looking for funding for any number of activities (many companies, in fact, prefer to issue bonds rather than go to a bank for a loan). Within corporate bonds there are two significant classifications:

▶ **Investment-grade Bonds.** These are bonds issued by top companies. The companies offering these bonds are seen as very financially secure. So these bonds are considered to be financially reliable.

▶ **Junk Bonds.** Also known as high yield bonds, these are put out by companies that don't have the financial solvency of investment-grade firms. With many junk bonds, there's a chance that the company will fail to live up to its agreement to repay bond holders. Given that risk, these bonds generally have a higher yield than other corporate bonds.

How Can You Tell the Difference?

The bottom line of a bond's financial security is its rating. Ratings agencies such as Moody's and Standard and Poor's assign a letter rating which summarizes the creditworthiness of the company selling the bond. For instance, at Standard and Poor's, they break down as follows:

▶ **AAA TO BBB.** These, starting with AAA, are the highest investment-grade bonds around. AAA is considered "extremely strong," while BBB is described as facing "major ongoing uncertainties."

▶ **BB TO B.** More risky than the first group, although Standard and Poor's says B-rated bonds show enough current strength to meet their obligations. Anything that

Useful Terms

Some other bond terms to know:

• **Coupon Rate.** A bond's specified interest rate.

• **Discount.** This is a bond that's being sold for less than its par value.

• **Face Value (also known as par).** The value of the bond as stated on the certificate or instrument.

• **Premium.** A bond that's being sold for more than its face value.

for that amount of time and interest rates go down, that sort of bond becomes exceedingly attractive. Again, however, the story's the same with jumps in interest rates. If you're holding a long-term bond that's paying, say, two percentage points less than other bonds, you'll take a bath if you try to sell it.

Where Bonds Can Fit

Given their function and advantages, bonds can fit any number of investment goals:

▶ **Savings.** If you have cash lying around that you need to park for the short term, something like a Treasury bill may offer higher rates of return than other types of savings.

▶ **Diversification.** Not only can bonds generate profits via interest rate movement, they can also offer diversification. For instance, keeping a portion of your portfolio in bonds can help soften the blow of drops in the price of stocks.

▶ **Income.** Since bonds pay interest to investors at regular intervals, they can be useful as sources of regular income, particularly for retirees looking to supplement other funds.

▶ **Tax-Free Income.** Provided you're in a high enough tax bracket, the tax breaks offered by such bonds as municipals can be significant.

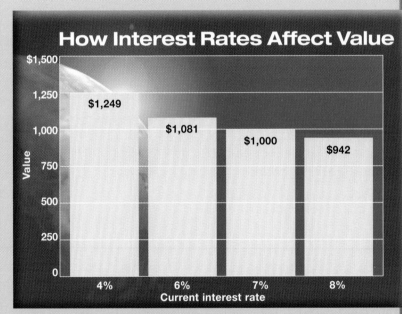

How Interest Rates Affect Value

To illustrate how a bond is affected by interest rate movement—and how investors can profit or lose money as a result—here's a chart that illustrates the effects of interest rate shifts. In this example, a $1,000, ten-year bond bought at a 7 percent interest rate is worth $101 more if interest rates drop to 6 percent. Should interest rates fall further to 4 percent, an investor would realize a $269 profit. But, if interest rates go up by one point to 8 percent, an investor would only be able to sell the bond for $962.

▲ Look to bonds for diversity, income, and possible tax advantages.

▼ Be aware that rising interest rates can hurt the value of bonds.

The Risks of Bonds

Like any investment, bonds also have their share of risks. It's important to get a feel for these risks, as they can influence what place bonds may have in your portfolio.

Downsides to Consider

Interest Rate Risk

This is one of the most significant risks of bonds. As we've seen, should interest rates go up, the bond you're holding drops in value because investors can now obtain bonds with higher interest rates. The longer the term of your bond, the more its value is affected by higher interest rates.

Credit Risk

As we noted with corporate bonds, a bond's financial strength is another issue to consider. While some bonds have top ratings and are considered very secure, those with less than stellar ratings can encounter all sorts of financial problems. That, in turn, may mean problems with meeting interest payments on time or, even worse, an inability to pay at all. That can spell the loss of your investment.

Know, too, that a top-rated bond isn't a sure thing by any means. Bond ratings can change as a result of developments in a company's financial position. That means a company—and its bond—that seemed solid last year may now be a good deal riskier.

Call Provisions

If you think of refinancing your mortgage when interest rates drop, then it shouldn't be surprising that companies do the same thing with bonds. This brings into play a bond's call provision, meaning that the company will pay off the bond before its maturity date. Many companies do this when interest rates fall, since they can reissue new bonds at a lower interest rate. Of course, you the investor are also faced with reinvesting your money at a lower interest rate as well.

Inflation

Inflation—increasing prices that erode the buying power of your money—is another important risk to consider with bonds. If you own a bond paying 7 percent and inflation is running at 3 percent, that means you're effectively getting only a 4 percent return on your

Liquidity Warning

Liquidity may not seem like much of a concern, but it has hurt bond-holders in the past. For instance, in the mid-1980s when interest rates were rising—often sharply—bond owners often had a hard time getting a decent price for their older bonds since their relatively low interest rates made them unattractive to potential buyers.

investment—nothing to write home about. Although bonds can grow in value with interest rate movement, stocks are historically better at beating the effects of inflation.

Liquidity

This is not a problem if you plan to hold onto a bond until maturity, but something to bear in mind otherwise. Liquidity refers to the ability to sell your bond quickly and at a fair price. While bonds such as U.S. Treasuries are very liquid because of their financial strength, you may encounter problems trying to sell other types of bonds, such as a bond issued by a financially troubled company that has recently been downgraded by one of the major ratings services.

30-Year Bond and CPI-U

All Items less food and energy

All Items

30 Year Bond

1994 1995 1996 1997 1998 1999 2000 2001 2002

To get a feel for how much inflation can impact a bond's yield, this chart shows the yield of the 30-year Treasury Bond and the inflation rate (as represented by the Consumer Price Index—All Urban, from 1994 to the present). Although the 30-year bond is no longer issued, it served as a market benchmark and is an ideal illustration of the effects of inflation on bond yields.

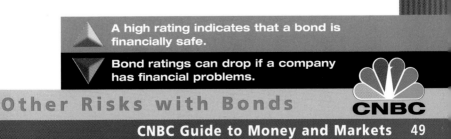

A high rating indicates that a bond is financially safe.

Bond ratings can drop if a company has financial problems.

Other Risks with Bonds

CNBC

How to Buy and Track Bonds

If bonds seem a worthwhile addition to your overall investing strategy, here are some guidelines for buying bonds and subsequently tracking their progress.

Ways to Buy Bonds

There are a number of ways to buy the various sorts of bonds sold to investors:

▶ **Full-service Broker.** Like stocks, you can also buy all sorts of bonds at a full-service brokerage house. But, as is also the case with stocks, you're going to pay a commission, an expense that eats into the value of your investment from the start.

▶ **Discount Broker.** As with stocks, it's less expensive to buy bonds at a discount brokerage house. You can also research and buy bonds at brokerage houses' online websites.

▶ **Direct Purchase.** You can also buy Treasury bonds directly from the federal government. These are offered at auction at regularly scheduled intervals and are available through a program known as Treasury Direct. To find out more, contact the nearest Federal Reserve Bank or check online at www.federalreserve.gov and www.treasurydirect.gov.

Laddering

One bond-buying strategy that can protect you from changes in interest rates is called laddering. This involves buying bonds that mature in sequence— say, for instance, bonds maturing in one year, three years, and ten years. With laddering, if interest rates go up, you'll have funds to invest at higher rates once the shorter bonds mature. And, if rates go down, the longer term bonds ensure that you'll still receive relatively high interest.

Tips for Buying Bonds

▶ **Shop Around.** For one thing, not every broker offers every sort of bond. For another, prices can vary from one place to another, so compare prices.

▶ **Check for Call Provisions.** If you're concerned about a bond being called before it matures, check the bond's prospectus (the legal document that describes the bond in detail) to see if the bond can be called and the earliest date at which that could happen.

▶ **Diversify.** Like you would with stocks, spread your bond holdings around. Don't own all the same sorts of bonds—as is the case with stocks, if you own too much of the same thing, you're vulnerable to a big hit.

Buy Bonds Like Stocks—Watch the Cost

▶ **Watch for Wrinkles.** As happens with other investments, there are all sorts of variations on the theme with bonds. For instance, if you're concerned about the effects of inflation, the Treasury now sells an inflation-indexed type of bond whose value is adjusted to compensate for inflation.

How to Track Bonds

If you want to track bonds in the newspaper, here are some things you'll need to know:

▶ Like stocks, newspapers list bonds in columns. Reading left to right, the first thing you'll see is the name of the bond's **issuer**.

▶ Right next to the name is the bond's **coupon rate**—the interest rate the bond was paying when the bond was first issued.

▶ Right after that is a two-digit number referring to the year in which the bond **matures**.

▶ The next column is the bond's **current yield**.

▶ After that, the **volume**, which shows how much the bond was traded the prior trading day.

▶ The next column—the **close**—is the last price the bond was sold for at the end of the last trading day. This is the price someone was willing to pay for the bond in relation to 100. For instance, a bond at 95 is trading at 95 percent of its par value.

▶ The last column—**net change**—reports how much, if any, the bond gained or lost in value.

▶ NOTE: Some corporate bonds trade on the stock exchanges while others trade over the counter.

Questions: Bonds, General

What is a bond?

What's the difference between a bond and a note?

Why are bonds considered less risky than stocks?

What are the historical rates of return for cash, bonds and stocks and how should they affect how my assets are allocated?

What's the difference between a bearer bond and a book-entry bond?

What is a callable bond?

How do I know if a bond is callable?

How will I know if my bond is called in?

What are taxable bonds?

How am I charged for buying or selling a bond?

View all Q&A for General

Watch expenses when buying bonds.

You may have to go to a brokerage house to find the bond you want.

and Be Sure to Diversify

CNBC

Mutual Funds—An Introduction

For many investors, mutual funds are the leading choice in their portfolios. And with good reason. As we'll see, mutual funds offer a dynamic variety of choices, providing investors with a range of opportunity and options unlike most other kinds of investments.

Funds Under the Microscope

Mutual Funds—What They Are

While many other investments involve only one entity—a stock, for instance, is an investment in one particular company—a mutual fund can encompass any number of investments and financial choices at the same time. A mutual fund is an investment company that pools money from many people and invests it in stocks, bonds, and other securities. Each investor owns shares which represent part of these holdings.

A Little History

Mutual funds may be all the rage these days, but they're by no means a recent innovation. The first mutual fund—Mass-achusetts Investors Trust—was organized in 1924. Investors could buy into the fund with a minimum investment of $250, although the privilege also carried a 5 percent sales charge.

Why Mutual Funds Work

It's no wonder that there are now thousands of mutual funds from which to choose. Here's an overview of some of their major advantages:

▶ **Diversification.** For many investors, it's difficult or impossible to diversify adequately among investments. Mutual funds, on the other hand, do this automatically—every dollar invested is effectively divvied up among all sorts of investments. That greatly reduces investment risk.

▶ **Professional Management.** Although picking your own stocks is something that many prudent, knowledgeable investors do all the time, it's not something everyone wants to do. A mutual fund offers professional investment management backed by research and experience.

▶ **Cost Efficiency.** This, of course, differs from one fund to the next, but it's no great task to find a fund that offers solid returns at a genuinely affordable cost to investors. By contrast, buying and selling the amount of stocks and other investments a fund routinely handles

Mutual Funds Offer Diversification and

would be prohibitively expensive for most investors.

▶ **Customization.** Again, since there are so many to choose from, there are funds to fit most any sort of investment goal. There are funds that load up on stocks, while others diversify among a holding of bonds.

Some Downsides to Consider

Mutual funds, like anything else to do with investing, aren't perfect. Here are several potential negatives to bear in mind:

▶ **Involvement.** Unlike choosing your own investments, mutual funds mean you're leaving decisions on strategy and implementation to someone else. That's fine for many investors, but others prefer a more hands-on role in managing their financial future.

▶ **Expense.** Not every fund is a bargain. As we'll see later, it's essential to choose a fund that operates in a genuinely cost-efficient fashion. Otherwise, you're just throwing money away.

▶ **Philosophy.** It may be surprising, but not every fund does precisely what it says it's going to do. Again, we'll cover this in detail, but it's also important to find a fund with a solid investment philosophy that it follows to the letter.

▶ **Performance.** Many funds consistently underperform their peers and marketwide benchmarks such as the Dow Jones Industrial Average.

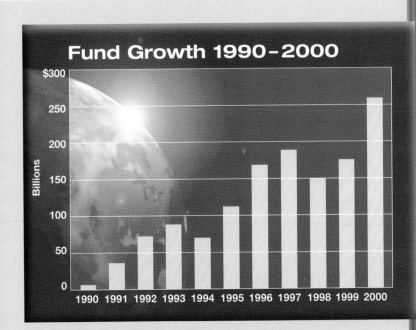

Fund Growth 1990–2000

To illustrate how mutual funds have exploded in recent years, this chart represents the flow of new investments into mutual funds from 1990–2000.

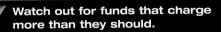

▲ Seek out cost-effective funds with a consistent philosophy.

▼ Watch out for funds that charge more than they should.

Professional Management

Stock Funds— Part One

Now that we have a feel for what mutual funds are as well as what their advantages and occasional drawbacks are, it's time to start wading into the various types of funds from which investors can choose. Note that the heading of this portion of the book refers to stock funds—we'll tackle the topic of bond funds in a subsequent section.

Major Stock Fund Types

Here's an overview of some of the major sorts of stock funds, how they differ from one another, and how different investors might view them. Funds in this group are defined primarily by how aggressive they are.

Aggressive Growth Funds

▶ WHAT THEY ARE: Aggressive growth funds generally invest in stocks from companies that have a real chance of taking off, such as small companies that are developing products and services which, hopefully, will be in great demand in the future.

▶ A GOOD MATCH FOR: Investors who are taking a long-term perspective with their money, since they'll need to ride out volatility. A suitable choice for young investors in something such as an IRA or other retirement account.

▶ A BAD MATCH FOR: Investors with a shorter time frame—say, someone trying to piece together a house down payment in the next five years—should steer clear of these. So should investors who don't have the stomach for what can prove a rough ride.

Growth Funds

▶ WHAT THEY ARE: Like aggressive funds, these funds are looking for growth opportunities, but they tend to go with more stable, established companies that, while showing plenty of potential for further growth, have more of a track record in place. Growth funds' returns may not be as high as those achieved by some aggressive funds, but the fall off the cliff isn't so steep if things go sour.

▶ A GOOD MATCH FOR: Investors looking for long-term growth, even these funds are slightly more conservative. They're particularly suited to investors who want long-

The Balanced Approach

Balanced funds are neither purely stock, nor purely bond funds. Rather, balanced funds strike a mix between the two, usually somewhere in the vicinity of 60 percent stocks and 40 percent bonds. With that sort of equitable diversity, balanced funds can be an ideal choice for an investor who's genuinely concerned about risk, but doesn't want to completely bypass exposure to stocks.

term growth potential but haven't the stomach for the wild ride proffered by more aggressive funds.

▸ A BAD MATCH FOR: Investors who want to avoid risk, as growth funds do carry a fair degree of volatility.

Index Funds

▸ WHAT THEY ARE: Index funds try to match the rate of return of major indices, such as the Dow Jones Industrials. So, for instance, if the Dow is earning 10 percent a year, an index fund manager will select a portfolio of Dow Jones stocks that will hopefully match that return.

▸ A GOOD MATCH FOR: Anyone who would be satisfied with matching the major barometers of the market (in addition to the Dow Jones, there are a number of other indices that can be tracked by index funds). In recent years, index funds as a group have outperformed other types of funds, a fact that argues for going with the flow rather than buying and selling a great deal in hopes of beating the rest of the market.

Another plus—since index funds tend to buy and hold more than other funds, they also have lower operating expenses, which puts more of their returns in your pocket.

▸ A BAD MATCH FOR: Investors who think that it's silly not to try to beat the overall market. And, in down markets, index funds will likely follow the tide and drop as well. By contrast, other sorts of

Do Index Funds Win?

One argument that has raged for years is whether it's better to go with an index fund or to try to do better with a more actively managed fund. The data below shows, over the past five years, how often managed equity funds have beaten the Standard and Poor's 500 Index:

	S&P 500 Return (%)	Funds that Beat the S&P (%)
2000 (single year)	-8.6	70.8
1998–2000 (three years)	13.9	40.3
1996–2000 (five years)	18.6	23.7

Source: Morningstar.com

mutual funds may be able to buck the downward trend.

Growth and Income Funds

▸ WHAT THEY ARE: Something of a hybrid. On the one hand, such funds usually invest in growth companies. However, Growth and Income Funds also put a portion of their money into more stable investments, such as established stocks that pay a large dividend. In that sense, the funds can also be a more conservative source of regular income.

▸ A GOOD MATCH FOR: Conservative investors who are more worried about not losing any money than in taking extreme risks in the hope of landing a big return.

▸ A BAD MATCH FOR: The investor who's willing to risk some volatility. And a mix comprising solely growth and income funds may be too conservative for the investor with a long-term outlook.

Look for a fund that matches your goals and comfort level.

A fund that's too aggressive for your style will only work against you.

Types of Stock Funds— Part Two

In the prior section, we covered major types of mutual funds, discussing their goals and willingness to be aggressive. Here, we'll move on to consider other types of funds that target specific types of stocks. We'll also examine types of funds that further break down the classifications of funds covered earlier.

More Groupings of Stock Funds

Many funds are a bit more specific when it comes to the types of companies in which they'll invest. They include:

International Funds

▶ WHAT THEY ARE: International funds invest in companies that are located outside the U.S. Some funds focus on companies in so-called "emerging growth" areas (countries that, historically under-developed, are beginning to advance economically), while others may also mix in bonds from overseas firms and governments.

▶ A GOOD MATCH FOR: Aggressive investors who don't want to limit themselves to the ups and downs of the domestic market.

▶ A BAD MATCH FOR: Conservative investors, particularly those who may be leery of political and economic instability overseas.

Sector Funds

▶ WHAT THEY ARE: These funds invest in stocks within a particular industry or economic sector, such as high technology, health care, or utilities. By concentrating their stock purchases, sector fund managers hope to score big if the industry as a whole is doing well.

▶ A GOOD MATCH FOR: Aggressive investors, particularly those who may be familiar with the sector in which the fund is investing.

▶ A BAD MATCH FOR: Investors who are diehard believers in diversification, since a sector fund limits itself to one particular area.

> ### Size Changes
>
> One thing to be aware of with regard to funds that focus on company size is that they can be highly mercurial. For one thing, as companies grow, many funds continue to keep them in their portfolios, even though they may no longer fit the fund's size parameters. Know, too, that funds define company size differently—a small-cap company in one fund may be classified a mid-cap by another fund.

Company Size Can Also Play a

Funds Built According to Company Size

Other sorts of funds focus on the size of the company in which they're investing. They include:

▶ SMALL-CAP FUNDS. These invest in relatively small companies, usually those worth less than $1 billion. These funds aim to get in on small companies on the ground floor. A subcategory is micro-cap funds, which deal in particularly small companies.

▶ MID-CAP FUNDS. These target companies with capitalization between $1 billion and $7 billion; they still look for growth but not with the extreme approach taken by small-cap funds.

▶ LARGE-CAP FUNDS. These focus on large, stable companies and de-emphasize growth potential; they also look for good dividend sources.

Further Within the Small-, Mid-, and Large-Cap Worlds

As can be seen in the chart below, some small-, mid-, and large-cap funds can be further broken down into those that target specific sorts of stocks, not just company size. Included in this grouping are such funds as growth, value, and blend funds. (Refer back to the section on stocks for the definition of a value stock. A blend fund invests in stocks of varying sizes and growth potential.)

To Index or Manage?

To further the examination of the index fund vs. managed fund debate, here are some additional numbers on how certain defined funds performed against index funds.

Active vs. Passive Management in 2000

Category	Actively Managed Funds Avg 2000 Return (%)	Index Funds 2000 Return (%)
Large-Cap Growth	14.10	14.06
Mid-Cap Growth	7.12	4.23
Small-Cap Growth	5.57	6.00
Large-Cap Blend	6.37	8.24
Mid-Cap Blend	3.81	0.80
Small-Cap Blend	13.53	9.77
Large-Cap Value	5.99	0.03
Mid-Cap Value	17.63	6.70
Small-Cap Value	17.47	15.20

Source: Morningstar.Com

Sector funds and international funds let you concentrate your investments.

Don't sacrifice diversification for too much focus.

More Stock Funds

Here is a look at a few additional types of mutual funds. Unlike the funds already covered, these are rather specialized, both in the way they operate and with regard to the stocks in which they choose to invest.

Three Other Types of Funds

Here are three more mutual funds that, at the very least, are worth knowing something about:

Exchange Traded Funds (ETF)

These have many features that are similar to conventional funds, but offer certain additional elements.

▶ WHAT THEY ARE: An exchange traded fund is similar to a conventional mutual fund in that they both represent a basket of stocks that can be bought or sold in a group. Each share of an ETF, like a mutual fund, represents a portfolio of stocks.

Buy a Bear?

So-called "bear funds" are another type of mutual fund. Unlike conventional funds that look to invest in companies with bright growth prospects, bear funds short stocks and use other strategies in the hope that the market will go down. They may work on occasion—for instance, as of summer 2001, the Prudent Bear Fund had a 37 percent 12-month gain—but the overall upward movement of the market usually means poor results for these funds.

▶ HOW THEY WORK: Like an index fund, ETFs are designed to mirror an index or other grouping of stocks. ETFs go by a number of names, including SPDRs (these follow the S&P 500 Index), Qubes (these track the 100 largest nonfinancial companies in the Nasdaq) and others.

▶ HOW THEY'RE DIFFERENT: ETFs differ from conventional mutual funds in several ways:

PURCHASE. While mutual funds can only transact business at the end of the trading day, exchange traded funds can be bought or sold at any time.

TRADING STRATEGIES. Unlike a mutual fund, an ETF can be sold short and bought on margin.

▶ WHERE TO FIND THEM: Large investment companies offer ETFs. Almost all ETFs are traded on the American Stock Exchange. (Notably, Qubes now also trade on the NYSE.)

Socially Responsible Funds

These seek to combine profit with the personal values of some investors.

▶ WHAT THEY ARE: Socially responsible funds stick to companies that the funds deem to be of reputable social value. That means some funds will avoid investing in companies dealing in nuclear power, alcohol, tobacco, firearms, and other similar activities.

▶ HOW THEY WORK: Many funds employ various "screens" to examine companies, not merely for their financial strength but for their adherence to certain types of social values.

▶ HOW THEY'RE DIFFERENT: Green funds frequently bypass companies that conventional funds would happily include in their portfolios. That raises a central argument about socially responsible investing:

Advantages. Supporters say that green funds invest in companies that are less likely to get into legal or environmental problems which can harm profitability.

Drawbacks. Critics say socially responsible funds cannot be as profitable as other funds since they avoid profitable companies because of certain aspects of their business.

▶ WHERE TO FIND THEM: A number of fund families specialize in green funds.

Funds of Funds

These, unlike conventional mutual funds, avoid individual stocks and bonds.

▶ WHAT THEY ARE: Funds of funds take proceeds from investors and, in turn, invest that money in other mutual funds.

▶ HOW THEY WORK: Like a regular fund, only with other funds. For instance, a growth fund will invest in other funds that concentrate most of their portfolios on growth stocks.

▶ HOW THEY'RE DIFFERENT:

Advantages. One advantage of funds of funds is greater diversification—rather than a group of stocks owned by the fund, investing in other funds provides a particularly broad array of holdings.

Drawbacks. One problem with funds of funds is the greater cost to the investor. Instead of paying fees for one fund, some funds of funds layer expenses from the other funds in which they invest.

▶ WHERE TO FIND THEM: A number of fund families offer funds of funds.

More Types of Funds

Collaborative Funds. Also known as collective intelligence funds. While these are managed by professionals, they choose the makeup of the portfolio based on recommendations from volunteer stock pickers. The idea is that the person on the street—not Wall Street—knows what's happening with stocks.

Hedge Funds. These, only open to investors with a substantial sum of money to invest, engage in everything from buying stocks to shorting stocks to trading in currencies. Since they have relatively few investors, they're also less regulated than conventional funds.

Precious Metals Funds. These funds invest in commodities such as gold and silver. These generally perform well only in times of severe inflation, since gold and silver are seen as buffers against increases in the cost of living.

Real Estate Investment Trusts (REITs). These are companies that invest in property such as apartment buildings, shopping centers, and other commercial ventures. Good for investors who want to get into real estate without the headache of investigating individual properties.

▲ Certain specialty funds can meet the needs of some investors.

▼ Keep an eye on costs and whether the funds may be too narrow in scope.

Broaden Investors' Choices

CNBC

Choosing a Mutual Fund

It's been said that choosing a good mutual fund is something of a game of chance, as you can never be sure what will happen from one year to the next. There may be a grain of truth to that, but there is still an array of pragmatic ways to evaluate mutual funds and determine which ones may be best for you.

Selection Basics

Here are some basic guidelines that are essential to consider when examining a mutual fund:

Performance

Naturally, everyone wants to find a winning fund. But it's important to define performance a bit more thoroughly so you have a complete sense of how a fund has done:

▶ **Long-Term Performance.** Don't just look at one or two years; see how a fund's performance has held up over the long haul.

▶ **Performance Consistency.** See how the fund has done from year to year. A fund that's returned 25 percent a year may sound great, but that may mean 50 percent one year and zero the next. That may be too volatile for some investors.

▶ **Performance Comparison.** Check to see how a fund has done in relation to similar funds. Again, a fund may have great-sounding numbers, but they'll pale if you find out other similar funds are performing much better. This data is available at CNBC on MSN Money's funds center. Performance data are also published in various newspapers and magazines. Ratings firms which rank mutual funds include Morningstar and Value Line.

Risk

Risk is a two-edged sword. On the one hand, inherent risk is one element that, in the end, results in profits for investors. On the other, too much risk is something that an investor needs to watch out for:

▶ **Standard Deviation.** This term refers to performance consistency. Look at the returns a fund has produced from year to year and see how the numbers compare. The broader the range, the greater the deviation, meaning that the fund has a higher degree of risk than others with more consistent returns.

Know Your Manager?

The issue of fund management is a topic of some controversy in the investment world. Some say it's absolutely essential to get to know fund management—after all, if he or she leaves, what might happen? Others contend that a fund's philosophy is far more critical. So, while management may be critical to one investor, it need not be for another. It all depends on which argument you buy.

> **Portfolio Mix.** Know the mix of a fund's investments. A fund that's almost exclusively weighted to stocks is likely going to be riskier than one with a greater allocation to bonds and cash. Taking that a step further:

> **Portfolio Breakdown.** Know precisely what the fund is investing in. Get a sense of the fund's investment philosophy as well as the specific stocks it's buying. As is the case with buying individual stocks, you may know that some of the stocks that the fund is choosing manufacture terrible products.

Expenses

We'll cover this topic in more detail later, but suffice it to say here that what a fund costs is an essential consideration. Look for:

> **Loads.** These are expenses that you pay to buy shares in a fund. By comparison, no-load funds don't levy this sort of charge.

> **Fund Expenses.** The day-to-day cost of running a fund—expenses that are ultimately passed along to you, the investor.

Other Considerations

Mutual fund performance is measured in many ways. It is a good idea for you to understand these measurements before investing. CNBC on MSN Money will help you with your studies. In the meantime, here are a few terms to get you started:

> **Standard Deviation.** Following up on the issue of performance consistency, standard deviation is a number that calculates how volatile a fund is—put another way, how likely it is that a fund will swing from positive to negative results in a given year. The higher the standard deviation, the greater the risk a fund carries.

> **Sharpe Ratio.** Developed by Nobel Prize winner William Sharpe, this takes standard deviation into account to further quantify a fund's riskiness. The higher the ratio, the better a fund's performance versus the risk it runs to obtain those returns.

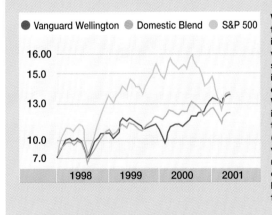

When we talk about performance consistency, it's ideal to find a fund whose growth is steadily increasing, year in and out. Here's one example, the Vanguard Wellington fund. While its performance is lower than the S&P 500 Index (it's a relatively conservative fund), it's nonetheless notched consistent growth that's better than its peer funds.

Look for steady, consistent performance.

Watch for funds that fly one year and plummet the next.

More Issues to Consider

Having gotten some global fund considerations in hand, it's time to consider more specific elements that go into choosing a winning mutual fund.

Fees, Taxes, and More

There are further specific elements that go into choosing a winning mutual fund. Here's a rundown of some more specific, critical issues to take into account:

Loads

A load is an expense to buy into a fund, pure and simple.

▶ WHAT THEY ARE: Commissions paid to brokers, financial planners and anyone else who sells you a load fund.

▶ HOW BIG CAN THEY GET? Loads can range upward of 8 percent of the amount of money you're investing.

▶ VARIATIONS ON THE THEME: Some loads are imposed at the time you buy into a fund (known as a front load). Others are levied when you sell (known as a back load).

▶ THE BOTTOM LINE: There's really no compelling reason to buy a fund that levies a load. Not only is it an added, unnecessary expense, but there are plenty of no-load funds that perform just as well as any load fund around.

▶ MORE PROBLEMS: Another potential pitfall with load funds— like any commission-based product— is that the salesperson may be pushing it to grab a commission, not necessarily because it's the right fund for you.

▶ WHAT TO DO: Stick with no-loads. They're cheaper and every bit as profitable.

Expenses

The expense of running a fund is something completely separate from a load.

▶ WHAT THEY ARE: Expenses are the costs of running a fund, including administrative expenses, paying fund employees' salaries, and other costs. These are subtracted from any returns paid to investors.

▶ HOW BIG CAN THEY GET? Expenses range all over the board, from next to nothing to several percentage points (a fund's expenses are expressed in the form of an expense ratio. For instance, a fund with a 2.0 expense ratio subtracts $2 in expenses from every $100 invested in the fund.)

Managing Taxes

Since taxes can be an important element in selecting a fund, a few funds advertise themselves as tax-managed funds. These funds try to limit their tax bite as much as possible by minimizing capital gains and dividends. But, be sure to compare these carefully, as a fund with a higher tax bill may still beat one with a lower tax payout if its returns are high enough.

There's No Compelling Reason

▶ THE BOTTOM LINE: It may not seem like much, but even a half-percentage point difference in expenses can mean a huge difference in a fund's ultimate profitability to investors.

▶ WHAT TO DO: Check a fund's expenses carefully, watching out for hidden costs. As a general rule of thumb, the closer you can keep a fund's expenses to 1.0 percent (ideally, even less than that) the better.

Portfolio Turnover

How much a manager moves a fund's holdings around can also affect how much you the investor receive in total return.

▶ WHAT IT IS: Portfolio turnover represents how much buying and selling a fund does. It's usually expressed as a percentage of the size of the fund—a 100 percent turnover, for instance, means the fund has completely changed its portfolio.

▶ WHAT IT MEANS: Portfolio turnover can be a useful tool in evaluating a fund. For one thing, a high turnover rate may suggest that a manager isn't satisfied with the portfolio and is consistently fiddling with it. Also, high turnover funds often have higher expenses than other funds.

▶ THE BOTTOM LINE: High turnover isn't always bad—for instance, there are a number of small-stock funds that do quite well by moving in and out of positions. But studies show that funds often perform better the lower their portfolio turnover.

Tax Efficiency

▶ WHAT IT IS: How much a fund pays out in taxes from the profits it generates. These derive from a fund's income as well as capital gains distributions from sale of stock in the portfolio.

▶ WHAT IT MEANS: Another important consideration because these, like other types of expenses, affect how much investors actually earn from a fund.

▶ THE BOTTOM LINE: Check out these performance elements:

Tax-Adjusted Return. This shows how much a fund actually returns after taxes. (Note: As of spring 2001, all funds must disclose their after-tax efficiency in prospectuses and annual reports.)

Tax-Efficiency Ratio. This number, which is computed by dividing after-tax returns by pretax returns, shows how efficient a fund is in relation to taxes. The scale runs from 100 (most efficient) on down, as tax efficiency declines.

Doing the Math on Loads

Loads, no matter what the fund, are always a hole that an investor has to dig out of before making a profit. To illustrate this, consider a load fund and a no-load fund—you buy 500 shares at $30 a share in each and add another $100 every month. They're the same in terms of growth rates (5 percent a year in share price), and management fees (1 percent a year). The only difference is a 1.25 percent front load. At the end of 5 years, you come out ahead with the no-load fund (23.37 percent return after taxes, versus 22.47 for the load fund). For help in calculating the impact of loads, try the load calculator at www.finsights.com/calculators/ calculators.ASP

▲ Tax efficiency can mean greater profits for a fund.

▼ Unnecessarily high expenses can drain a fund's profitability.

Some Final Mutual Fund Issues

Having covered the major elements that go into choosing a mutual fund, here are a few final topics that warrant some consideration.

Still More Mutual Fund Considerations

Asset Size

When it comes to mutual funds, bigger is not necessarily better.

▶ THE ISSUE: How much money a fund handles can have a large effect on how the fund operates and, in turn, how well investors in the fund fare.

▶ WHAT CAN HAPPEN: A large influx of investors' money into a fund may impact the stocks a fund chooses. For instance, a fund may try to specialize in small stocks. But, with a lot of money to invest, it's often difficult to buy large blocs of small stocks cost-effectively and efficiently.

▶ WHAT TO WATCH FOR: Keep an eye out for funds whose asset size has doubled in the last year or so. Many funds, in fact, will shut off sales to new investors so they can keep themselves at a manageable size.

Closed-End Funds

Up to now, we've been discussing open-end funds. Closed-end funds operate in a different way.

▶ THE ISSUE: Open-end funds sell an unlimited number of shares based on investor demand. Closed-end funds issue only a certain number of shares. Also, open-end funds buy back investors' shares—shareholders of closed-end funds sell their shares to other shareholders on an exchange.

▶ WHAT CAN HAPPEN: Both open-end and closed-end funds are broken down according to net asset value (the value of one share). However, since a closed-end fund is traded on an exchange, the actual price you will pay for a share will differ from the net asset value—you'll probably pay a premium if the fund is doing well, while you may get a discount on shares if the fund is doing poorly.

Longevity Check

If you're interested in a large fund family, try to find out how long the average fund manager's tenure happens to be. In many cases, managers in large families that do well with smaller funds are quickly promoted to larger, more important funds. That can limit how long top-flight management is likely to stick with any one fund.

▸ WHAT TO WATCH FOR: If you can buy shares at a discount, profits can come from two sources—increase in net asset value if the stocks within the fund do well and additional growth in NAV as demand for the fund increases.

Families

This term refers to a company that offers a number of different funds.

▸ THE ISSUE: Rather than a bunch of autonomous funds, most funds are grouped according to families. This is a collection of funds that are released and managed by the same firm.

▸ WHAT CAN HAPPEN: The number of funds in a family can range across the board. Some companies only have one fund while some—such as the mutual fund giant Fidelity—can offer hundreds of funds.

▸ WHAT TO WATCH FOR: The size of a fund family can cut both ways. Small fund families often have excellent track records because management only has to concentrate on a limited number of funds. But a large fund family not only offers a greater amount of variety in the funds it offers, it often reduces or waives fees if you move money between funds within the family. A large fund family can often make record keeping easier, as you can receive consolidated statements.

Research Sources

Having covered various elements of what goes into choosing a mutual fund, here's a list of places to track down this information:

Prospectus. Every fund publishes a prospectus in which the fund's management specifies investment goals, performance statistics, and facts covering fees, expenses, and other data.

Annual and Semiannual Reports. These can provide significant updates to information presented in the prospectus. For instance, annual and semiannual reports offer updates on what has changed in a fund portfolio.

Online. CNBC on MSN Money provides a wealth of data and statistics on mutual funds. Type in a fund's ticker symbol and investors can access performance charts, expense information, details on fund management, and analysts' expectations regarding a fund's future performance.

Publications. Financial newspapers and magazines regularly have articles on mutual fund performance. There, readers can get information on fund size, tax efficiency, and how funds have performed in comparison with similar funds.

▲ A large fund family can offer services that smaller ones cannot.

▼ Particularly fast growth in asset size can hurt fund performance.

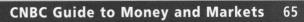

How to Buy a Mutual Fund

This section will cover various ways to buy mutual funds as well as certain considerations to bear in mind when investing in a particular fund.

Getting into a Mutual Fund

Like individual stocks, there are a variety of ways to buy mutual funds.

Stockbrokers

Like stocks, you can always go to a stockbroker—either full-service or a discount house—to buy almost any mutual fund available. The downside is you'll pay extra to buy the fund, particularly if you opt for the full-service broker.

Online Brokers

These, while offering the immediate convenience of research and account access, are likely to be less expensive than conventional full-service brokers. You still need to open an account and deposit funds to execute trades, however.

Direct from the Funds

This is perhaps the easiest way to buy the fund you want. If you've decided on a fund, contact the fund family, either by phone, mail, or through the company's website. Once you contact the family, they'll send you an application and a fund prospectus (for faster turn-around, you can also download applications and a prospectus directly from the website). Read the prospectus, complete the application, write your check, and return it to the fund company.

Mutual Fund "Supermarkets"

This is a recent phenomenon in the world of mutual fund investing. Rather than limiting itself to a particular fund family, a supermarket offers one-stop shopping for funds from various fund families. Many even waive fees if you move your money from one fund family to another. The major disadvantage is that they can be a more expensive place from which to buy funds, as the "supermarkets" charge fund families extra fees for listing them—charges that are passed along to investors.

Less Paper

Another advantage to a mutual fund supermarket—particularly as your investments grow and you buy into different funds—is consolidated paperwork. Rather than having to juggle statements from different fund families, most supermarkets will summarize all your activity in the same statement. That's handy, especially at tax time.

How Small Can You Start?

The issue of minimum starting investment can be a problem with some mutual funds. Here, we show a sampling of some top-performing domestic mutual funds over the past ten years, along with the minimum investment necessary to get started in the fund.

	Ten-year total return	Minimum initial ($)
1. Fidelity Select Home Finance	23.44%	2,500
2. Fidelity Select Financial Services	21.89%	2,500
3. Calamos Growth A	21.63%	500
4. Davis Financial A	21.02%	1,000
5. Smith Barney Aggressive Growth A	20.70%	1,000

Other Mutual Fund Purchase Issues

Where to buy mutual funds isn't your only consideration. Bear in mind other aspects of getting into—and staying in—a solid mutual fund.

Investment Minimums

It may be surprising to some investors—after all, funds should be more than happy to accept your money—but it's difficult, if not impossible, to buy into some funds. For one thing, as we noted earlier, certain funds cut off sales to hold down the overall size of the fund.

Perhaps of importance to a greater number of investors, most funds have a minimum initial investment. This can range anywhere from a modest amount—$50 or so—up to tens of thousands of dollars or even more.

If getting into a fund requires more money than you have at one time, some funds let you buy into a fund if you set up an automatic investment program. This,

usually involving a bank account or some other similar account, lets the fund withdraw funds on a regular basis.

CAVEAT: Be careful where your money goes with these sorts of automatic investment programs. Some funds will put the money right into the fund you want, while others will stick it in some sort of low-interest account until you accrue enough to reach the fund minimum.

Auto Invest

No matter if you have enough money to get into a fund or need to set up an automatic withdrawal program, it's a great idea to get an automatic investment program in place sooner or later. Again, this usually involves establishing an automatic withdrawal program with another account. Not only does this put your investing on autopilot, it also lets you take advantage of dollar-cost averaging, a system discussed earlier that can cut your cost of investing.

Automatic Investment Plans are a great way to watch your holdings grow.

Some funds have a prohibitive minimum investment.

Tracking Your Mutual Funds

Now that you've bought into a mutual fund or two, here are some techniques and strategies for staying on top of them.

Ways to Follow a Fund

In Print

No matter if it's a major financial publication or your local newspaper, print media is one handy way to stay abreast of your mutual fund holdings. While specific fund listings will differ from one publication to another, here are some symbols, abbreviations and terms to bear in mind. In fact, you'll likely hear some of this terminology in all sorts of media.

Format

Funds in print are listed under the heading of the fund family. From there, funds are listed in alphabetical order. Reading left to right, here are some common elements:

▶ **Fund Name.** This is always listed first.

▶ **Footnotes.** Next to the name you may see some letters. These have the following meanings:

b —the fees that pay for the fund's marketing costs come from fund assets.

d—you'll pay a deferred sales charge or a redemption fee when you sell the fund.

f—a front-load sales charge is in effect.

m—multiple fees are charged.

p—the previous day's net asset value.

s—the fund split its shares yesterday.

x—fund paid a distribution yesterday.

NAV. The net asset value of the shares. Shares are sold to the pub-

---

A Steady Watch

One valuable rule of thumb in tracking a mutual fund is don't over-react to the daily ups and downs of the market. Any fund—no matter how conservative—is going to have some movement, so that's no cause for panic. However, you should become concerned if long-term trends begin to develop, such as a fund consistently underperforming similar funds or indices. If that's the case, do some homework—maybe the fund has a new manager or the fund has changed its investment philosophy.

---

lic at NAV, plus any sales charge and are redeemed at NAV, less any redemption charge.

▸ **Daily % Return.** One-day total return.

▸ **YTD % Return.** Total return, year to date (calculated from December 31 onward).

NOTE: Other publications and media may provide additional details than those offered by the format explained above. For instance, some may include additional performance data covering three years, five years, and other time frames. Information on sales charges and a fund's expense ratio may also be included in listings. Certain publications may also use some sort of quick reference system—a letter or other symbol—as an easy way to determine how a fund has performed in relation to its peer funds.

Online

Thanks to the Internet, you can also follow your funds via a variety of online news sources. As a sample, here's how you can track a fund with CNBC on MSN Money:

▸ Type in the ticker symbol for the fund.

▸ You'll then go to a page that summarizes recent fund activity, including net asset value, daily price change, year to date return, and other information.

▸ From there, you can click to obtain additional fund information, including customized charts, detailed return information, the fund's top holdings and other information.

▸ CNBC on MSN Money also brings you up to speed with regard to recent significant developments that may impact the fund's performance. Click on "fund review" for information on management style, changes in the fund's overall strategy and, ultimately, how an analyst feels about the fund's past performance and prospects.

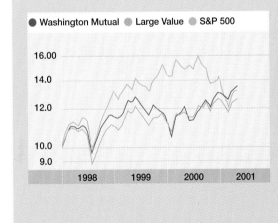

● Washington Mutual ● Large Value ● S&P 500

Web sites like CNBC on MSN Money offer many ways to research and follow mutual funds. You have access to fund descriptions and analysis by ratings companies like Morningstar. You'll also be able to compare the performance of your fund to other funds and benchmarks like the S&P 500.

It's important to follow your fund's progress closely.

Don't overreact to daily fund volatility—that's par for the course.

Other Mutual Funds—Bond Funds

Like stocks, a portfolio of bonds can be selected and overseen by professional management. Here's an overview of bond funds and how they may fit into an investor's portfolio.

Bond Fund Basics

Here's a rundown of some essential features of bond funds.

What They Are

Like a stock fund, bond funds come in many types:

▶ **Corporate Bond Funds.** These invest in bonds issued by companies. As is the case with individual bonds, corporate bond funds cover the waterfront, ranging from solid, highly rated issuers to more risky junk bond funds. The higher the risk, the greater the potential return.

Do Tax Savings Pay?

Just as you would with individual municipal bonds, check to see if a municipal bond fund's tax advantages pay off. For instance, a fund yielding 5 percent bought by someone in the 28 percent tax bracket would earn the taxable equivalent of 6.9 percent (5 divided by .72). So a taxed investment paying 6.9 percent or higher is a better deal.

▶ **Government Bond Funds.** These invest in bonds issued by the federal government. They cover short-term, intermediate and long-term U.S. government bond funds. The longer the term, the higher the return, but also the greater the interest rate risk.

▶ **Municipal Bond Funds.** Like their individual counterparts, these comprise bonds issued by municipalities to pay for various sorts of projects. They're exempt from federal taxes. For buyers of single-state funds, income is also free of state and local tax if the investor lives in that state.

▶ **Foreign Bond Funds.** As the name implies, these invest in overseas bonds, primarily those issued by foreign governments.

Advantages

Bond funds offer a number of advantages when compared with individual bonds:

▶ **Diversification.** Rather than putting your money into one bond, a bond fund offers investors immediate diversification. That can be particularly important, given bonds' relationship to interest rates and how quickly bonds can be affected by interest rate movement. Fund diversity minimizes this risk.

Bond Funds Offer Management

▶ **Portfolio Diversity.** Like individual bonds, bond funds can offer additional diversity when coupled with stocks or stock mutual funds.

▶ **Management.** Like stock funds, you're under the leadership of professional management in buying and selling bonds.

▶ **Income Flow.** Compared with individual bonds that only pay twice a year, bond funds pay investors interest every month. That makes them ideal for investors who need some cash flow.

▶ **Liquidity.** Unlike individual bonds that can sometimes be difficult to sell quickly, it's easy to withdraw funds from a bond fund or to sell your holdings completely.

Drawbacks

Bond funds have one overriding drawback—since the fund is comprised of various bonds, there's no preestablished maturity date. That means, should you sell the fund, what you'll get depends on the net asset value of the overall fund at that time. That can be less or more than what you paid, depending on how interest rates have moved.

Bond Fund Investments

Like stock funds, investor interest in bond funds has also boomed in recent years. This chart illustrates the growth of assets in bonds from 1995 to 2000. Bonds account for 11 percent of all assets held in mutual funds.

Source: The Investment Company Institute

▲ Bond funds offer more consistent income flow than individual bonds.

▼ Like individual bonds, don't assume tax-free is necessarily the best strategy.

and Diversity

How to Choose a Bond Fund

Bond funds share a number of characteristics with stock funds. It's important to bear these in mind when shopping for a suitable fund.

What to Look for in a Bond Fund

Here are a number of factors that should be considered when evaluating bond funds.

Performance

▸ **Look at long-term performance.** As is the case with stock funds, pay particular attention to the fund's long-term return record—no shorter than, say, five years.

▸ **Look at both the fund's yield as well as its total return.** Yield is the amount of compounded monthly dividends that the fund pays out to its investors—couple that with price movement (whether the fund's price went up or down in reaction to interest rates) and you get the fund's total return.

Expenses

The issue of how much you're paying to buy into a bond fund is no less important than it is with stock funds. Look at how much you'll be charged for owning a particular bond fund. As a general rule, it's hard to justify investing in a bond fund which charges a high management or sales fee.

Maturity

This gives you an excellent idea of just how the fund will react to interest rate movements. If, for instance, the fund has lots of bonds that have a relatively short-term maturity (say, in the neighborhood of five to ten years), the fund will not react as badly to interest rate increases as a fund that's heavy in long-term maturity. In particular, look for a term known as weighted average maturity—this statistic is the average of all the bonds in the fund.

Open or Closed?

Like stock funds, bond funds also come in two primary varieties—open end and closed end. Open-end bond funds have an unlimited number of shares. In contrast, closed-end bond funds have a limited amount of shares and trade on an exchange. That means closed-end bond funds usually trade at a premium or discount from their net asset value.

Loads

Bond funds come in two types—those sold by someone who gets a commission for the sale, and no-load funds that don't cost you a dime upfront. Go with the no-loads—you'll save money right off the bat.

Minimum Initial Investment

Different sorts of bond funds require different minimums to get started. Some require as little as $100, while others mandate as much as $25,000. But bond funds are also available via an automatic investment program. So, if a bond fund or family interests you, call their 800 number and see what they have in the way of getting started inexpensively.

Portfolio Turnover

Stock funds usually don't benefit from a portfolio that's in flux too much—the same holds true for bond funds. Not only can a fund run into trouble by trying to predict interest rate movement—for instance, buying short-term bonds for fear that interest rates will rise—but funds that are managed to excess are often unnecessarily expensive for investors.

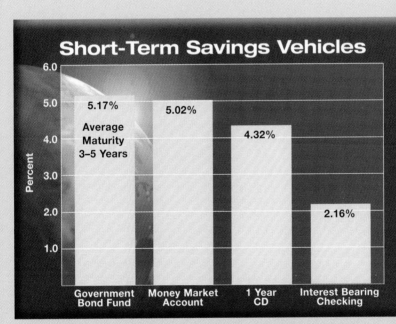

Short-Term Savings Vehicles

- Government Bond Fund: 5.17% (Average Maturity 3–5 Years)
- Money Market Account: 5.02%
- 1 Year CD: 4.32%
- Interest Bearing Checking: 2.16%

How an investor uses a bond fund depends on temperament and goals, but one useful application is as a spot to park cash for the short term. Check out the following returns for various types of short-term savings vehicles. Granted, the bond fund may be the riskiest of the four, but the extra income over the short term may be worth it.

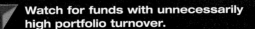

▲ Bond funds can be an ideal spot to park short-term cash.

▼ Watch for funds with unnecessarily high portfolio turnover.

Would a Stock Fund

CNBC

Money Market Mutual Funds

If you're looking for a suitable spot for your savings—or a place to put money that you ultimately intend to invest—money market mutual funds are worth a look.

Money Market Mutual Funds

Money Market Basics

▶ WHAT THEY ARE: Money market mutual funds are, in fact, a form of mutual fund. Unlike stock and bond funds, however, they're much more conservative. Money market funds generally invest in investment-grade government and corporate debt with short terms, such as CDs, commercial paper and bankers' acceptances.

Low Risk

Although the risk of a money market mutual fund isn't make-believe, it should not be a consuming concern. For one thing, if you buy a money market from a large mutual fund company, there's virtually no chance that the fund is going to fail—larger fund families have the financial means to cover any sort of shortfalls. And, while some money market funds have, on occasion, dropped a bit in value, the fund companies have always been there to make up the difference to ensure that the $1 per share price has held.

▶ HOW THEY WORK: Unlike stock and bond mutual funds, the net asset value of a money market mutual fund never changes. As such, the net asset value is generally $1 per share and stays there.

Advantages

▶ **Higher Interest Rates.** Since they're actually investing in things paying a reasonable return, money market mutual funds pay a higher interest rate than comparable savings vehicles such as Certificates of Deposit and bank savings accounts.

▶ **Liquidity.** It's easy to get your money from a money market mutual fund. In fact, most funds provide check-writing privileges for that very reason.

Drawbacks

▶ **Risk.** Again, since the fund is technically investing in something else, a money market mutual fund is not guaranteed as bank savings accounts are. That means—theoretically, at least—there is the chance that you can lose money in a money market fund. If that is of concern to you, you may want to opt for a savings vehicle with iron-clad security.

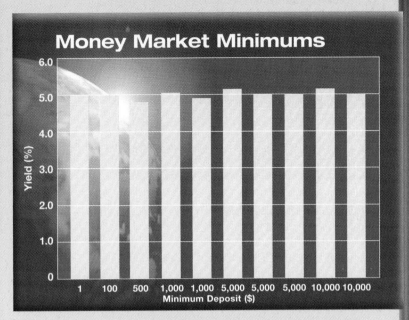

Money Market Minimums

Yield (%) — vertical axis: 0, 1.0, 2.0, 3.0, 4.0, 5.0, 6.0

Minimum Deposit ($): 1, 100, 500, 1,000, 1,000, 5,000, 5,000, 5,000, 10,000, 10,000

Do money market funds with higher minimums pay higher interest rates? Not really. To illustrate why it pays to shop around for the best deal—both in terms of rates of return and the money you have to commit—here's a chart of yields for 10 funds and the minimum deposits they require.

What to Look for

▶ **Yield.** This number usually differs from the quoted "rate" that a fund is paying. This refers to the fund's compounding function—the fund is paying dividends on the money you have in it, which, in turn, generates additional return. Pay attention to the yield when shopping for a money market fund, since it tells you more accurately what your money will earn in a particular investment.

▶ **Withdrawal Limitations.** While money market mutual funds offer check writing privileges, some may impose restrictions on the amount an investor can withdraw. For instance, some funds require no less than $100 or so per withdrawal. If you expect to use the fund in relatively small amounts, make sure the fund's minimum withdrawals allow you to do so.

▶ **Starting Minimums.** Like other sorts of mutual funds, there's also the issue of the minimum you have to have to open an account. Some fund families require you to deposit as much as several thousand dollars to get into a money market fund. However, as is the case with their other products, fund families also let you set up an automatic withdrawal program that can get you into a money market with nothing down and $50 or so taken automatically from an account you designate.

▲ Money market funds pay higher rates than savings accounts.

▼ Unlike bank deposit accounts, money market funds are not guaranteed.

Certificates of Deposit

Certificates of Deposit offer another alternative to low-paying savings accounts and interest-bearing checking accounts.

The Lowdown on CDs

Certificates of Deposit (CDs) offer investors yet another place to put their money—either as a savings vehicle or as a place to put cash that they eventually plan to invest in something else.

How Certificates of Deposit Work

▶ WHAT THEY ARE: Basically, CDs represent a savings contract between an investor and the institution selling the certificate of deposit.

▶ HOW THEY WORK: You give the institution (which can range from banks to savings and loans to brokerage houses) your money, and the funds are placed in a CD—a savings contract that pays a prespecified interest rate. The interest rate holds steady for the life of the certificate

of deposit, which can be as short as one month to as long as several years. At the conclusion of the CD's term, your principal is returned to you, plus any interest earned. Alternatively, you can also roll the money directly into a new CD.

Advantages

▶ **Safety.** Unlike other places to park cash, such as a money market mutual fund, CDs are guaranteed. That means, if the institution selling you the CD is backed by the Federal Deposit Insurance Corporation, the money you put into the CD is completely protected. Even if the bank or other institution that sold it to you collapses, you'll get your principal back.

▶ **Predictability.** While rates of return for money market mutual funds will vary, CDs always pay the rate that they specify. There's no guesswork or uncertainty involved.

▶ **Competitiveness.** Although CDs don't offer super-high returns, they are better than savings accounts, interest-bearing checking accounts, and, on occasion, short-term bond funds.

Drawbacks

▶ **Penalties.** Once you buy a CD, you're pretty much locked into it for the duration. Should you withdraw your money early, you can be hit with an early withdrawal

Avoiding Penalties

One way to protect yourself from CD penalties is to distribute your savings among several different CDs. That way, rather than being hit with a huge fine if you have to withdraw a large chunk of cash, you can access portions of your savings with lesser exposure to penalties.

CDs Offer Safety and Guaranteed

penalty. These generally range from three to six months' worth of interest that would have been paid had you held on to the CD.

▶ **Interest Rate Risk.** Here, investors run the risk of getting an inferior rate of return. If, for instance, you buy a CD at 5 percent and interest rates jump to 6 percent, you're stuck with the lower rate of return until the CD matures.

▶ **Automatic Reinvestment.** Unless you let the bank or other institution know otherwise, they'll automatically reinvest your money in a new CD after a CD matures. That can be a headache if you plan to use the proceeds.

What to Look for When CD Shopping

▶ **Know Your Rate of Return.** Banks and other issuers compound CD interest rates in all sorts of ways—some do it daily, others weekly, still others on a monthly basis. To know precisely what you're getting into, make sure to ask about the CD's annual percentage yield. This is the most meaningful way to compare one CD's payout with another.

▶ **Ask About Penalties.** Since these can range across the board, be sure you know how much you'll lose should you choose to cash in a CD prior to maturity.

▶ **Check Around.** You can find the best rates on CDs in publications such as *Money* Magazine and on websites such as Bankrate Inc.'s (www.bankrate.com).

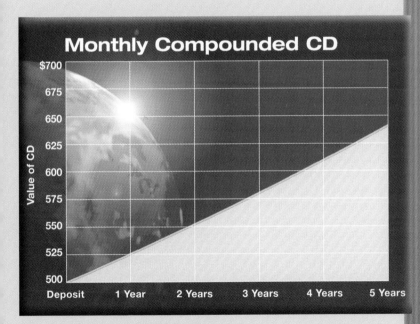

Monthly Compounded CD

Compounding comes into play with CDs, particularly CDs with long terms. To illustrate how this works, here's a graph which shows how much you would earn if you invested $500 in a five-year CD paying 4.98 percent, compounded monthly.

Certificates of deposit provide predictable returns.

Early withdrawals can bring stiff penalties.

Other Investments

Individual Retirement Accounts— Part One

You may think that constantly changing tax laws make IRAs a moot point for many investors. But, the fact is, an IRA can be an exceedingly effective element of your retirement plan. Moreover, recent changes in tax law greatly enhance their value to many investors.

Breaking Down the IRA

What It Is

The traditional Individual Retirement Account (IRA), initially put into law in 1981, let you set aside up to $2,000 of earned income in an account designated specifically for retirement. The new tax law permits contributions of $3,000 between the years 2002 and 2004. That increases to $4,000 between 2005 and 2007 and up to $5,000 for 2008. Thereafter, the limit will be indexed for inflation annually.

▶ WHAT'S CHANGED OVER THE YEARS: Lots. The original IRA let you deduct your contributions from your income (regardless of whether you had a retirement plan where you worked or not). Five years later, Congress tightened deductibility rules for IRAs. Ten years later, they reversed course yet again, restoring much of the traditional IRA's deductibility and introducing the so-called Roth IRA (see page 80).

▶ WHO CAN DEDUCT NOW: For a full breakdown of deductibility as of 2002, see the chart on the facing page. But, in a nutshell, new IRA guidelines have opened up deductibility to a great number of people—estimates hold that nine out of ten working Americans can take advantage of IRA deductions in some fashion.

Other Traditional IRA Features

▶ **Contribution Limitations.** The maximum annual contribution permitted to IRAs is $2,000 for the 2001 tax year (increasing to a maximum of $5,000 in 2008), or 100 percent of the individual's com-

Early Withdrawals

Happily, there are some exceptions that let you withdraw funds from a traditional IRA before you reach age 59½. They include: Paying for certain types of unreimbursed medical expenses; If you become disabled before age 59½; If you're the beneficiary of another IRA owner who has died; Buying, building, or rebuilding a first home; Paying for certain types of higher education expenses.

Traditional IRAs Offer Tax Deductions

pensation, whichever is lower. The source of the contribution to the IRA can come from anywhere. If you are 50 or older an additional, catch-up contribution can be made starting at $500 for 2002–2005 and rising to $1,000 for 2006.

▶ **Contribution Deadlines.** Contributions can be made to a traditional IRA at any time during the year or by the due date for filing your tax return. Put another way, this means that contributions for 2001 must be made by April 15, 2002.

▶ **Withdrawal Guidelines.** You cannot begin withdrawing money from a traditional IRA until you're at least 59½ years old (although there are some exceptions—see opposite). If you withdraw early you must pay a 10 percent penalty, plus income tax. By the same token, you must begin withdrawing money from a traditional IRA no later than age 70½. Also, no more contributions may be made after that point.

▶ **Beneficiary.** A feature of traditional IRAs lets you name a beneficiary who will receive the proceeds of your account should you die.

Advantages

▶ **Tax Deferral.** Although you often have to pay taxes on any money you withdraw from a traditional IRA after retirement (unless you made non-deductible contributions to a traditional IRA account), all money in an IRA grows tax-free until it's withdrawn. That greatly increases the growth of your retirement account.

▶ **Lower Tax Impact.** Although it's not true in all cases—as illustrated by the birth of the Roth IRA—you may benefit from a tax standpoint through a traditional IRA's tax deferral feature. The reason for this is that an investor will likely be in a lower tax bracket once he or she has retired, thereby lessening the tax bite on IRA funds that are withdrawn.

▶ **Ease and Flexibility.** It's simple to set up a traditional IRA—just fill out a form and deposit your contribution. Moreover, how you choose to invest your IRA is entirely up to you—you can be as aggressive or conservative as you wish. (We'll look at some suggestions for IRA investment strategies later.)

Can I Take a Traditional IRA Deduction?

Adjusted Gross Income of Under:	If You Are Covered by a Retirement Plan at Work and Your Filing Status is:		
	• Single	• Married Filing Jointly • QualifyingWidow(er)	• Married Filing Separately
$10,000	Full	Full	Partial
$31,000	Full	Full	None
$41,000	Partial	Full	None
$61,000	None	Full	None
$81,000	None	Partial	None
$150,000	None	None	None
$160,000	None	None	None
$160,000 or over	None	None	None

This chart summarizes whether certain people can deduct a full or partial traditional IRA contribution. For similar information if you are not covered by a retirement plan at work, and for more fine print details from the IRS, visit http://www.irs.gov/forms_pubs/graphics/15160x01.gif

▲ You can withdraw IRA funds early for certain exceptions.

▼ You may pay a 10 percent penalty for an IRA withdrawal.

and Tax-Deferred Growth

CNBC

Individual Retirement Accounts— Part Two

To further the benefits and options offered by Individual Retirement Accounts, investors may also consider the Roth IRA.

All About Roth IRAs

In 1997, Congress approved the IRA Plus—also known as the Roth IRA, named after Senator William Roth of Delaware, chairman of the Senate Finance Committee that directed a series of tax law changes.

What They Are

▶ **Contributions.** Singles making up to $95,000 a year, and couples making up to $150,000, are eligible to contribute as much as $2,000 for the 2001 tax year, even if they're taking part in a retirement program at work. As with traditional IRAs, maximum contributions will rise to $3,000 for 2002–2004, $4,000 for 2005–2007, and $5,000 for 2008. Catch-up provisions for those over 50 also apply.

▶ **No Tax Deductibility.** Unlike conventional IRAs, Roth IRAs offer no provisions at all for any sort of tax deduction for deposits.

▶ **Tax-Free Withdrawals.** As opposed to traditional IRAs, where withdrawals are taxed, all proceeds from Roth IRAs may be withdrawn tax-free if you're over 59½ and the money has been invested for over five tax years.

▶ **Early Withdrawal Penalties.** Roth IRAs and traditional IRAs have similar penalty structures. For instance, any withdrawals made before age 59½ carry a 10 percent fine, plus income tax.

▶ **Early Withdrawal Exceptions.** Like a traditional IRA, Roth IRAs let you withdraw funds early under the same set of circumstances, such as buying a first home or paying certain medical expenses.

▶ **Beneficiary.** As is the case with a conventional IRA, Roth IRAs require that you name a beneficiary

The Beneficiary

Whether using a Roth or the more traditional type of IRA, give careful thought when deciding on a beneficiary. One good rule of thumb is to name a spouse, if possible. Not only does that let your spouse roll over your account into his or her own IRA, a new beneficiary can also be named. This prolongs the life of the IRA and effectively extends the time before withdrawals have to be made.

Roth IRAs Offer Different Features Compared

Plus and Minuses: A Comparison

Here's a chart summarizing the advantages and drawbacks of Roth IRAs.

On the plus side: No tax consequences at all when you start to withdraw funds.
On the downside: Loss of any sort of tax deduction for any contributions made into the account.

On the plus side: No requirement mandating withdrawals from the account after a certain age.
On the downside: As opposed to the tax advantages of traditional IRAs, Roth participants are effectively using after-tax dollars to contribute to their accounts.

On the plus side: So long as you're earning income and meet other guidelines, you can theoretically continue to contribute as long as you like.
On the downside: Choosing to convert a traditional IRA into Roth has immediate tax consequences.

On the plus side: Under certain circumstances, you can withdraw funds early without penalty.
On the downside: Political uncertainty. Those who worry that the government may tinker with the provisions of the Roth IRA may want to stick with the more traditional IRA.

who will receive the proceeds of your account in the event you die.

Advantages

▶ **Tax-Free Growth.** As is the case with conventional IRAs, Roth IRA accounts grow tax-free.

▶ **Tax-Free Withdrawals.** As noted above, distributions from Roth IRAs are completely tax-free.

▶ **No Mandatory Withdrawals.** Unlike traditional IRAs that require participants to begin withdrawing money no later than age 70½, Roth IRA participants may wait as long as they wish to begin taking money out of their accounts.

▶ **No Cutoff to Contributions.** Provided an investor is earning income and meets certain other guidelines, Roth IRA participants can continue to make contribu-

tions into accounts for as long as they like.

Drawbacks

▶ **Loss of Tax Deductibility.** Although the tax-free withdrawal feature of Roth IRAs is attractive, some investors might benefit more from the tax deductibility of traditional IRA contributions.

▶ **Tax Consequences.** We'll discuss this in greater detail in the section addressing IRA conversion but, should you decide to change from a traditional IRA to a Roth IRA, you pay income taxes on the amount of money you're transferring.

▶ **Other Penalties.** If you take money out within five years of opening a Roth, you're subject to a 10 percent penalty plus taxes on any earnings.

▲ Roth IRAs let you withdraw money tax-free after you retire.

▼ If you need an immediate tax break, Roth IRAs do not provide it.

with Conventional IRAs

CNBC

Choosing the Right IRA

Now that we've laid out the various features of both traditional IRAs and their Roth counterparts, here are some issues and strategies to bear in mind when deciding what type of IRA to open (and whether it's a good idea to change from the one you may already have).

Account Considerations

If You're Opening an IRA...

Should you be on the verge of opening an IRA, here are some suggestions to help you choose between traditional and Roth IRAs:

▶ **If you don't qualify for an upfront deduction on a regular IRA, opt for the Roth.** The reasoning is easy—with the traditional IRA, not only do you not get any sort of tax break on the contribution, but you're taxed on the earnings when you start withdrawing the money on the other end. With Roth, you get the benefits of tax-deferred earnings plus tax-free withdrawals.

▶ **On the other hand, if you're in a high tax bracket now and expect that it'll be lower once you retire, consider the traditional IRA.** If you can get the deduction, it may do you more good now than tax-free withdrawals further on down the line.

▶ **If you're in a relatively low tax bracket now but expect it to go up as you get older—or, alternatively, you expect to stay pretty much in the same tax bracket— choose the Roth.** Tax-free withdrawals in a relatively high tax bracket make a world of sense.

▶ If you expect you may need money from an IRA within the next several years, avoid a Roth.

As noted on the prior page, any money taken out within five years of opening a Roth account results in taxes and penalties.

If You're Thinking About Converting a Traditional IRA into a Roth...

Before we tackle conversion issues, know that there are certain conditions that prohibit a conversion of a traditional IRA into a Roth:

▶ If you're married but filing separately for tax purposes.

▶ If your adjusted gross income (single or married) is greater than $100,000.

Partial Conversions

Know, too, that there is a middle course between the traditional IRA and the Roth. In some cases, it makes sense to convert a portion of your conventional IRA. Not only can that limit the tax consequences of conversion, it also earmarks a portion of your retirement funds for the tax-free advantages of a Roth.

If, however, neither of those apply, consider when giving thought to conversion:

▶ If you're not sure whether you'll need IRA money when you retire—or don't know how soon you may need those funds— change over to a Roth. Unlike the traditional IRA, you're not required to withdraw a penny.

▶ Likewise, if you see your IRA as part of your estate that you will want to pass along to your heirs, choose the Roth as well. Again, a Roth gives you more leeway to keep your IRA intact.

▶ If you plan on working in some capacity, it's probably sensible to choose the Roth, as you can keep making contributions regardless of your age.

▶ Planning to live life to the fullest—money-wise, at least— after you retire? The Roth may be the way to go. If you're going to be withdrawing significant funds to underwrite a fancy lifestyle, accessing that money tax-free will probably work to your advantage.

▶ On the other hand, if you're in a low tax bracket, the Roth's tax-free withdrawals are not as worthwhile as for someone in a higher bracket (especially given the cost of conversion and loss of tax deductibility that come with moving to a Roth).

▶ Likewise, if you expect to pay a significant tax bill to convert to a Roth, you may want to put up with the tax implications of a regular IRA. Be particularly careful if you actually have to use IRA funds to pay the taxes—that can only result in more penalties.

Roth Versus Traditional IRA

Here's one illustration of why it pays to be thorough when deciding between a Roth IRA and a traditional IRA. In this scenario, even though the Roth IRA lets you avoid taxes when withdrawing funds, it's better to stick with the conventional IRA.

Which is Better: Regular IRA or Roth IRA?

Because it will provide you with $3,517 per month during retirement, the deductible IRA will provide more retirement income than your other options.

	Investment Type	
	Deductible IRA	Non-Deductible IRA
Lump Sum at Retirement Before Tax	$595,254	$363,715
Lump Sum at Retirement After Tax	$459,115	$289,881
Monthly Retirement Income	$3,517	$2,209
Savings At Death	$15,683	$15,485
	Roth IRA	Taxable Investment
Lump Sum at Retirement Before Tax	$363,715	$128,751
Lump Sum at Retirement After Tax	$363,715	$128,751
Monthly Retirement Income	$2,782	$889
Savings At Death	$15,621	$15,326

▲ The 10 percent early withdrawal penalty doesn't apply when converting an IRA to a Roth IRA.

▼ If conversion taxes are prohibitive, stay with the traditional IRA.

Other Types of IRAs

Although conventional and Roth IRAs make up the bulk of IRA accounts, there are other types of IRAs that are worth having a look at.

Two Other Types of IRAs

Simplified Employee Pension (SEP-IRA)

▸ WHAT IT IS: Formally known as a Simplified Employee Pension Retirement Account (SEP-IRA), this is a program for self-employed people and small-business owners.

▸ HOW IT WORKS: It's similar to a conventional IRA in that it's exceedingly simple to set up—usually only one page of paperwork. But, unlike a regular IRA, contribution guidelines are a good deal more liberal. Tax-deductible contributions can be up to 15 percent of compensation, as much as $25,500 for 2001 and $30,000 for 2002. The maximum compensation that can be considered is $170,000 for the 2001 plan year and $200,000 for 2002.

▸ OTHER FUNCTIONS: Like a regular IRA, you can contribute as late as the April tax filing deadline for the prior year (longer if you file an extension). And, as with a conventional and Roth IRA, SEP-IRA owners name a beneficiary who will receive the proceeds of their account should they pass away.

▸ WITHDRAWAL PENALTIES: An SEP-IRA has the same early withdrawal penalties as conventional IRAs. No withdrawals before age 59½ can occur without a penalty, and distributions must start no later than 70½. Like regular IRAs, SEP-IRAs have the same exceptions for early withdrawals.

Advantages

▸ **Fully Deductible.** All contributions to SEP-IRAs are fully tax deductible. Moreover, there are no income limitations as there are with other IRAs.

▸ **Greater Contribution Limits.** While IRAs limit investors to $2,000 in contributions ($3,000 for 2002–2004), SEP-IRAs allow for much larger yearly contributions.

▸ **Flexibility.** Participants can decide how much they'd like to contribute in a given tax year (although lower contributions can increase tax liability).

Drawbacks

▸ **Tax Impact.** Unlike the Roth IRA where proceeds are withdrawn tax-free, there is no escaping the tax impact of an SEP-IRA when you start withdrawing funds.

Education IRAs

▸ WHAT THEY ARE: Now formally known as Coverdell Education Savings Accounts (CESAs), these allow savings for a child's education. From 2002 they can be used for primary and secondary tuition costs as well as for college.

▸ HOW THEY WORK: Contributions of up to $500 (increasing to $2,000 for 2002) may be made in any given year, depending on income. Contributions may only be made for a child under age 18 and contributions are not tax-deductible.

▶ OTHER ELEMENTS TO EDUCA-
TION IRAs: The child who is the
named beneficiary controls how
the money is spent but is only
allowed to use funds for educa-
tional purposes.

▶ TAX IMPLICATIONS: Generally,
withdrawals are free of tax if they
don't exceed the amount of qualified education expenses for the
year.

Advantages

▶ **Tax-free Growth.** Funds in
Education IRAs grow tax-free.

▶ **Control Limitations.** Unlike
other types of savings vehicles in
which children are named beneficiaries, an Education IRA may be
used only for education, and not

for any other purpose the child
chooses.

Drawbacks

▶ **Mandated Withdrawals.**
Should a child decide not to go
to college, an Education IRA
cannot remain intact indefinitely,
continuing to grow tax-deferred.
Instead, all assets must be withdrawn by the time the account
beneficiary reaches age 30. However, it can be transferred to
another family member for edu-
cational uses, if that person is
under age 30.

▶ **Contribution limits.** Contributions are limited to $2,000 per
year. As such, investors would
likely augment Education IRAs
with other sets of college savings
vehicles.

Investing Checklist

**No matter which type of IRA works best for you, here's a checklist
of issues to consider when deciding on a funding and investment
strategy:**

IRAs Are Generally Long-Term Investments. With few exceptions,
IRAs are something you'll own for a long time. This suggests a fairly
aggressive investment strategy. You'll likely have enough time to ride out
volatility and profit accordingly.

Remember to Diversify. Even though time is likely on your side with an
IRA, don't forget to diversify accordingly. Proper diversification across
various types of assets limits risk and boosts total return.

Try to Fund to the Max. Particularly with SEP-IRAs, where the more
you can contribute, the more you cut your tax bill, it's always a good
idea to contribute as much as you can to an IRA.

Fund, Even If You Don't Get a Tax Break. While the tax deductibility of
IRAs is a nice enticement, don't shortchange your contributions if you're
not eligible for deductions. That money is growing tax-deferred, something that really boosts your total return. Even better, with a Roth IRA that
money will be available to you tax-free when you start to withdraw it.

Don't Forget to Keep Your Risk Tolerance in Mind. Even with a time
frame that argues for aggressiveness, don't go against your comfort
level. You may end up doing more harm than good.

▲ **SEP-IRAs let you contribute large
amounts of money for retirement.**

▼ **Education IRAs impose rather limited
contribution levels.**

401ks—An Overview

It may be a surprise to some, but a powerful investing weapon is actually a workplace benefit—the 401k plan.

Introduction to 401ks

A 401k plan is an automatic salary-reduction and investment program.

How It Works

In essence, an employee agrees to have a certain portion of his or her paycheck automatically deducted on a regular basis. Employees' pre-tax contributions are limited to 12–20 percent of annual pay, or $10,500 a year, whichever is less. From there, the money is placed in an investment vehicle of their choosing. Depending on the type of 401k the company offers, that can be anything from mutual funds to company stock to bonds to money market funds. Starting in 2002, contributions limits increase $1,000 per year—from $11,000 in 2002 to $15,000 in 2006. Individuals over 50 can contribute an additional $1,000 per year in 2002, increasing $1,000 each year until the maximum of $5,000 per year in 2006.

Advantages

▶ **Automatic Deduction.** Rather than having to write a check to contribute to an ongoing investment program, a 401k takes care of contributions automatically.

▶ **Tax Advantages.** Technically, 401k contributions occur before the money is treated as income by the Internal Revenue Service. Not only can that result in significant tax savings, it also boosts the inherent return of the 401k program.

▶ **Tax-Deferred Growth.** Funds in 401k plans grow tax-deferred and are only taxed—like a conventional IRA—when funds are withdrawn.

▶ **Company Matches.** Depending on company policy, many employers "match" employee contributions. Some plans are generous enough that companies match employee contributions dollar for dollar.

▶ **Borrowing Privileges.** Many companies allow you to borrow from your 401k, usually up to half the money in the account with a maximum of $50,000. Interest rates are usually only a point or two higher than what you'd incur for a conventional loan, and loan terms are usually for five years.

▶ **Portability.** Taking into consideration vesting (see below) you can roll over all the proceeds from one 401k into another plan when you change jobs.

Drawbacks

▶ **Vesting.** This is the time allowed before company matches actually become the employee's

---

%, Not $

While many employees specify a dollar amount for regular contributions, see if you can earmark a percentage of your salary. That way, as your income increases, your 401k contributions will go up automatically.

The 401k—A Powerful Workplace

The Power of 401ks

Here's an illustration of how the advantages of 401k participation can quickly add up:

Assumption One: You deposit $3,000 into your 401k program every year.

Assumption Two: You're in the 15 percent federal tax bracket and 6 percent state tax bracket.

Assumption Three: Since the $3,000 you deposit in your 401k is not counted as taxable income, you save $450 on your federal taxes.

Assumption Four: Since the $3,000 isn't considered taxable income by the state, you save an additional $180.

Assumption Five: In tax savings alone, you have pocketed $630.

Assumption Six: The $3,000 you deposit into your 401k account earns a conservative 5 percent. That comes to $150.

Assumption Seven: Between federal and state tax savings and return on your investment, your $3,000 effectively generates $780.

Conclusion: Between tax savings and return, your $3,000 401k contribution generates a 26 percent annual return. Even more significant—if your deposits, tax brackets, and return hold true every year, that's a 26 percent return year in and year out.

property. This can take upwards of several years or, alternatively, may happen in increments. The idea is to motivate employees to remain with a company.

▶ **Investment Options.** 401k plans specify the investment options employees have. These usually include mutual funds, money market accounts, and company stock. On occasion, 401k plans can be rather limited in their investment options.

▶ **Sign-Up Limitations.** 401k plans are not necessarily available to employees immediately upon hiring. Depending on the employer's policy, you may have to wait as long as a year to join. Moreover, there are usually only certain times of the year when you can join a company 401k.

▶ **Early Withdrawal Penalties.** Like other retirement plans such as IRAs, 401k plans have penalties for withdrawals before age 59½—taxes plus an additional 10 percent fee.

▶ **Loan Payback Limitations.** If you leave a job or get fired while you have a loan out from your 401k, you have to repay the full amount quickly. Otherwise, the IRS considers the loan a withdrawal, with resulting taxes and penalties.

NOTE: If you work for a nonprofit organization or public school, you have access to a similar retirement vehicle known as a 403b. These are virtually identical to 401ks, but one major difference being that with a 403b you can contribute a slightly larger percentage of your salary than you can with a 401k (a bit more than 16 percent).

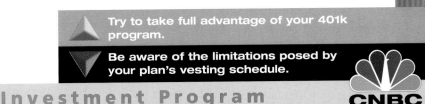

▲ Try to take full advantage of your 401k program.

▼ Be aware of the limitations posed by your plan's vesting schedule.

Employee Stock Options

This is yet another employee benefit that can prove lucrative to the individual investor—provided he or she knows precisely what employee stock options are and how to use them.

Understanding and Using Employee Stock Options

Employee stock options are part of many companies' compensation packages and can offer a useful way to build an investment portfolio or reap financial gains.

▶ WHAT THEY ARE: A stock option gives the employee the option of buying company stock at a particular price.

▶ HOW THEY WORK: Stock options in their essence are rather straightforward. Employees buying stock via a stock option hope that the shares will increase in price and that they can subsequently sell them for a profit.

In some cases, the exercise price that an employee pays for a stock option is lower than the fair market value of the stock (what the stock would cost on the conventional market). In these instances, employees have the option of exercising their stock options and selling the shares right away for a quick profit.

The Mechanics of Stock Options

Stock option programs consist of the following elements:

▶ **The grant date** is when your employer gives you the options to buy stock. This can last several years.

▶ Should you choose to buy the stock, this is known as **exercising** your options.

▶ The price you pay to exercise your options to buy stock is called the **exercise price**.

▶ The date after which you may no longer exercise your stock option is called the **expiration date**.

Strategies to Consider

Bearing in mind how stock options basically work, it's important to consider how to handle them effectively:

▶ Although stock options are designed as a profit incentive for employees, you may wish to pass on exercising your options if you're concerned about how the company's stock may perform in the future.

▶ On the other hand, if you're optimistic about the company, you may choose to exercise your options and hold the stock, hoping that the difference between what you paid to exercise your options and the fair market value of the stock will continue to increase— boosting your profit with it.

Different Stock Option Plans Have

Taxing Your Options

To illustrate how different stock option plans can result in different tax liabilities, consider the following scenarios:

Incentive Stock Options:

▸ An employee buys 500 shares of company stock through an incentive stock option plan. The exercise price is $20 a share. **Cost:** $10,000.

▸ Two years later, she sells the shares at $40 a share. That results in a profit of $20 a share. Total Sale Price: $20,000. **Profit:** $10,000.

▸ At a capital gains rate of 20 percent, that would result in a tax liability of $2,000. **Total profit: $8,000**.

Nonqualified Stock Options:

▸ An employee buys 500 shares of company stock through a nonqualified stock option plan. The exercise price is $20 a share. **Cost:** $10,000.

▸ The fair market value at the time the employee exercises his options is $30 a share. **Value:** $15,000.

▸ That means a difference of $5,000 at the time he exercises his options. At a 28 percent federal tax rate, that results in an immediate **tax liability** of $1,400 (28 percent times $5,000).

▸ Two years later, he sells the shares at $40 a share. That results in a profit of $10 a share between the $40 price at sale and the original market value of $30. **Profit:** $5,000.

▸ At a capital gains rate of 20 percent, that results in an additional **tax liability** of $1,000.

Total Profit: $7,600.

Note: Another element in the tax ramifications of stock options is called the Alternative Minimum Tax (AMT). This takes into account such things as deductions and whether the options had a greater market value at the time an employee exercises an option. In essence, you also have to calculate your tax liability under AMT to see if you might owe more. Check with an accountant for more details, but bear AMT in mind—many employees have been stunned to discover that they owe thousands more in taxes than they expected because of the AMT.

Tax Ramifications

Another aspect to consider is exactly what sort of stock option plan your company offers. They have very different effects on how much you may pay in taxes.

▸ **Nonqualified Stock Options.** With these, your taxes are broken down into two increments: First, on any difference between what you pay for the stock at exercise and the stock's fair market value, you will owe tax. Then, when you sell the stock, you may owe capital gains tax based on the difference between the fair market value at the time you exercised the stock and the price you get at the sale of the stock.

▸ **Incentive Stock Options.** Here, the tax is computed based on the difference between the exercise price and the price you receive when you eventually sell the stock.

▲ Employee stock options are a way to profit from a company's growth.

▼ Know what sort of stock option program is in place.

Places to Find Help

We touched on the topic of stockbrokers in an earlier section. Here, we go into more detail on what to look for with full-service brokers.

Picking a Full-Service Broker

As we discussed earlier, not everyone is comfortable going through the world of the markets alone. Here's a guide to shopping for and choosing a full-service stockbroker.

How to Decide

To get a sense of whether you need a full-service stockbroker, here are some issues to bear in mind.

▸ **How Independent Are You?** If you feel at home researching and tracking your investment decisions, there's really no need to pay extra for a broker's services.

▸ **How Much Service Do You Need?** There is more to this questions than meets the eye. If all you need is a means to execute trades, then a discount or online broker may be the way to go. However, consider these benefits as equally important elements of "full-service":

> Education—what do you want to learn from your broker?
>
> A broker can help minimize your tax bite.
>
> A broker can help you define investment goals.
>
> With a broker you can avoid mistakes, particularly those you have made in the past.

▸ **What Sort of Research Would You Like?** While many brokerage houses offer free research to all types of clients, many also provide proprietary information and research to full-service clients.

▸ **How Much Are You Willing To Pay?** The big question for many. Full-service brokers can levy expensive commissions—every time you buy or sell.

▸ **How Much Ongoing Guidance Would You Like?** A stockbroker doesn't have to be limited to just buys and sells—some track and monitor portfolios and client activity far more thoroughly than that.

What to Ask

If the guidance offered by a full-service broker seems appealing, keep these questions in mind:

▸ Ask what affiliations and memberships the broker has—is she registered with a state agency and the SEC?

▸ What special training or designa-

Getting Started

To start the search for a full-service broker, ask friends or colleagues for recommendations. Try to interview at least three brokers to get a feel for the varied philosophy and services that each may provide. One red flag to remember: never, ever deal with a broker who refuses to give you references.

Full-Service Brokers Offer Services That

tions does the broker have? (See the chart in the financial planners section for more information.)

▶ What sorts of clients does the broker have? What is their average age? Net worth? Investment goals?

▶ How much money does the broker manage? How long has the broker been in the industry?

▶ What's the broker's overall investment philosophy? Is the broker aggressive by nature or more concerned with protecting clients' assets?

▶ Does the broker have any expertise or particular experience in specific types of investments or industrial sectors?

▶ Exactly how will the broker be compensated? What is the broker's specific fee structure? Is there any sort of minimum purchase or minimum commission?

▶ What sort of returns has the broker's recommendations generated? Are there any statistics that you can use to compare the broker with other full-service brokers?

▶ What other guidance can the broker provide in addition to investment recommendations?

▶ Finally, can the broker provide you with a list of references, including clients with a similar background, temperament, and goals to yours?

Be On the Lookout

Unfortunately, you need a working knowledge of what can go wrong in a broker-client relationship. Here's a glossary of terms:

Breach of Contract. Some investors take action against full-service brokers based on perceived breach of contract. This can range from general mismanagement of an account to failure to follow a client's explicit instructions.

Churning. The common term for unnecessary trading or other activity within a client's account. For instance, a broker can be accused of churning an account to generate greater commissions.

Failure to Supervise. Brokerage firms are required by law to oversee their brokers to ensure that they are following proper regulations and are consistently acting in their clients' best interests. If not, a firm may be accused of doing an inadequate job of making certain that its brokers were following federal and other securities regulations.

Unsuitable Trading. Since brokers are required to make recommendations that are appropriate for clients, some may also be accused of providing improper investment advice. For instance, a retiree on a fixed income who was sold speculative growth stocks because they generated the broker a commission could claim unsuitable trading.

If an investor feels that she has been treated improperly by a stockbroker, she may file a complaint with state or federal regulatory agencies, including such organizations as the Securities and Exchange Commission and the National Association of Securities Dealers (NASD). From there, the investor may file legal action against the broker or take the issue to arbitration—the NASD, for instance, has an arbitration forum that serves as an alternative to the court system for solving client-broker disputes.

▲ **Be sure to ask a comprehensive series of questions when choosing a full-service broker.**

▼ **Don't do business with a broker who won't provide references.**

Are Attractive to Some Clients

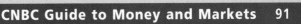

More Places to Find Help

Two alternatives to the cost of full-service brokers are discount brokers and online brokers. The cost may be less, but the guidance an investor receives can also differ.

Discount Brokers and Online Brokers

The distinction between these two terms has dulled in recent years. As such, they'll be grouped together in a common discussion.

▶ WHAT THEY ARE: Discount brokers—as the name implies—provide brokerage services at a cost that's generally less expensive than full-service brokerage houses. When discount brokers first began operating, that usually meant accessing discount services in person or via the telephone—now, discount brokers also provide products and services via Internet websites.

Blurring Lines

The distinction between online and discount brokers—not to mention full-service houses—is becoming less all the time. Full-service behemoth Merrill Lynch, for instance, now offers an online trading program at discounted commissions. By the same token, discount bellwethers such as Schwab have moved toward a full-service bent, providing investment guidance and advice for an additional charge or for free for clients with larger portfolios.

What They Offer

In general, whether over the phone or on the World Wide Web, discount brokers are characterized by the following:

▶ **Lower Commissions.** Compared to full-service brokers whose commissions can be exorbitant, discount brokers are downright cheap—often less than $10 for an unlimited number of shares and no matter what the overall value of the transaction.

▶ **Value Added Services.** Discount brokers also offer a variety of adjunct services and products, especially via their Internet sites:

Research. Some brokerage houses make research and analysis reports available to investors—others are more focused on an inexpensive means to buy and sell.

Portfolio Tracking. Websites offer portfolio tracking mechanisms, often providing up-to-the-minute stock and mutual fund prices.

News. Websites are useful for following current business, investing, and market news. Some offer interactive e-mail services through which clients can receive word of breaking news about a particular stock or mutual fund.

What Does the Market Say?

One way to get a sense of what sorts of conditions benefit certain types of brokerage houses is to look at the companies' stock performance. Here's a chart showing the annual rates of return for some discount and full service brokers, as well as their price to earnings ratios. When things were hot, less expensive brokers benefited from the boom in investor interest. When the markets settled back down, the more traditional full service houses more than held their own. Equally interesting is the effect of worldwide turmoil in the fall of 2001—sufficiently unsettling to negatively impact almost all of the brokerages.

Annual returns	1999	2000	2001*	P/E*
1. Ameritrade	313.1%	-67.7%	-9%	N/A
2. Etrade	123.4%	-71.8%	13.55%	N/A
3. Merrill Lynch	26.6%	65.5%	-23.18	17.89
4. Schwab	36.3%	11.4%	-47.5%	56.4

*Note: Statistics as of mid-2001.

Other Investments. Like their full-service counterparts, discount brokers deal in investments other than stocks and mutual funds, including options, initial public offerings, private stock placements, and money market accounts.

Issues to Bear in Mind

As you would when choosing a full-service broker, know what sort of an investor you are when choosing a discount service. If you feel confident enough to chart your own course, a discount broker can prove an effective addition to an overall financial program. But, keep these issues in mind:

▶ **Cheap, but at a Price.** With some exceptions, the inexpensive rates that discount brokers offer come at the expense of guidance. For the most part, discount brokers leave the investor on his or her own in making investment decisions.

▶ **Different Brokers for Different Investors.** While most any discount/online broker can pro-

vide cheap commissions, many are structured differently to best complement different kinds of investors. For instance, some have fee structures that are advantageous to active investors; others offer more services for investors interested in one-stop shopping for different products. Look around and compare.

▶ **Bricks and Mortar.** Some online brokers are purely Internet-based, others maintain actual offices. If it's important that you at least have the option of dealing face-to-face with a brokerage house, bear that distinction in mind.

▶ **The Power of the Dollar.** Although discount/online brokers may smack of pure investment democracy, that's not always the case. Some, in fact, offer services, discounted rates, and other goodies to investors with larger accounts and more assets. That said, if you can bring a lot of money to the table, check to see how much various brokers may offer in return.

Discount brokers offer greatly discounted commissions and fees.

With few exceptions, discounters don't offer full-service guidance.

Other Places to Find Help

If you're interested in particularly comprehensive financial guidance and advice, financial planners are another option worth considering.

Picking a Financial Planner

Many people might find it hard to distinguish a "financial planner" from other sorts of money professionals. But there are some differences that set planners apart—issues that investors do well to consider.

What They Are

Many planners are trained to oversee and guide an investor's financial life, often more broadly than a stockbroker or other sort of financial professional. This can include:

▸ Investments

▸ Budgeting and other day-to-day money-management matters

▸ Insurance

▸ Estate planning

▸ Taxes and tax planning

Write it Down

One final tip for dealing with financial entities and professionals: If you have a concern about what they do, or about their policies, fees, and other details, be sure that you have it put in writing. Not only can that prove valuable if something goes sour, but it can also be a warning flag—anyone or anything that won't put something down on paper likely isn't trustworthy.

What to Ask About

If the idea of a financial pro who can take a holistic view of your finances seems appealing, know that the financial planning industry is, as a whole, rather underregulated. While restrictions differ from state to state, in many places anyone can legally call themselves a financial planner. Bear in mind:

▸ **The Planner's Uniform Application for Investment Advisor Registration**, or **ADV**. Any planner federally licensed to give investment advice must complete this, which details how the planner earns her money, any connections with other firms and the sorts of investments recommended. Consumers can see information on about 9,000 advisors at www.adviserinfo.sec.gov.

▸ **Compensation.** Have any planner spell out how they expect to be paid. Some planners are on salary, others are paid hourly, while others receive some sort of commission-based structure.

▸ **Implementation.** Ask if the planner will put an investment program into place for you or if you're expected to do that. Again, that may be a function of licensing, as some planners legally can't buy any product they actually recommend. That may impact how much you eventually spend.

▸ **Investment Recommendations.** Unlike stockbrokers who may have a broad interest in a variety of investments, some planners limit themselves to the sorts of investments with which they'll work (such as mutual funds and nothing else). If your investment interests are broad, be sure to ask about this.

Other Shopping Tips

Depending on your situation, you may want to raise the following issues:

▶ **Other Persons.** If you're interested in a number of financial services such as tax and estate planning, ask if the planner handles that by himself, if they have someone else in the firm look after

it, or if they farm it out to someone outside their company.

▶ **Conflicts of Interest.** Depending on the various relationships a planner may have, he may be paid for recommending certain products from particular companies. Similarly, the planner may be paid for referring you to other professionals, such as tax preparers and insurance salespeople.

▶ **Disciplinary Problems.** Again, the ADV should cover this, but ask which organizations the planner belongs to, and contact them to see if the planner has ever been disciplined.

Letters of Distinction

Whether attached to a stockbroker, financial planner, or other financial pro, you often see a bunch of letters that designate some sort of special training or degree. Here's a glossary of what they mean:

Certified Public Accountant (CPA). An accountant who has passed an administered examination that focuses on accounting practices and taxes (not investments). CPAs must also be approved by state boards.

Certified Financial Planner (CFP). A financial planner who has passed exams accredited by the Certified Financial Planner Board of Standards, a regulatory body that sets CFP standards. The tests focus on an applicant's ability to work with clients' estate, insurance, investments, and tax affairs.

Chartered Financial Consultant (ChFC). A designation awarded by the American College, in Bryn Mawr, Pennsylvania, to financial planners who complete 10 courses and 20 hours of examinations covering economics, insurance, taxation, estate planning, and other related areas. They must also have at least three years of experience in the field of finance. (This is the insurance-industry equivalent of a CFP.)

Chartered Financial Analyst (CFA). Awarded by the Institute of Chartered Financial Analysts, this focuses on portfolio management and securities analysis. It also covers economics, financial accounting, portfolio management, securities analysis, and standards of conduct.

Registered Investment Advisor. Someone who has received approval from the Securities and Exchange Commission to give financial advice to clients for a fee.

Registered Representative. The official term for a stockbroker or account executive with a brokerage firm. To be registered, a broker must pass licensing exams administered by the National Association of Securities Dealers. Some states require additional testing.

▲ Financial planners often offer a broad range of services.

▼ Shop carefully—financial planners are woefully underregulated.

Would Any Financial Pro

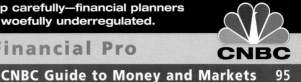

After-Hours Trading

While many investors might assume that buying and selling are limited to the operating hours of the stock exchanges, the advent of after-hours trading is changing how and when investors can implement their financial strategies.

How Trading After-Hours Works

In recent years, individual investors have been able to execute buy and sell orders after the markets have closed.

How Things Used to Be

Traditionally, institutions were able to trade stock no matter if the exchanges were actually trading or not. The essential issue was bringing buyers and sellers together, something that was far easier during trading hours.

What Changed

▶ **Electronic Investing.** Once markets moved more into electronic trading, it became easier for institutions to engage in after-hours activity.

▶ **Electronic Communication Networks** or **ECNs.** In particular, development of ECNs—electronic order matching systems—made it possible for brokerage houses to provide clients with access to after-hours trading. ECNs link buyers and sellers without the common point of an open market.

What Is After-Hours Trading?

After-hours—or extended—trading is real-time trading that takes place outside the normal exchange hours of 9:30 A.M. to 4 P.M. Eastern Standard Time. With after-hours systems, buyers and sellers may transact business before the markets open as well as after the markets have closed.

How It Works

Using ECNs, brokerage houses electronically match buyers and sellers to execute orders. Trades carried out after hours are processed as though they had been instituted during regular trading hours.

Limits Required

One requirement for many after-hours trading systems is limit orders—this means that investors must specify the exact price at which they will execute a trade before they can actually place the order. Given the limited numbers of buyers and sellers after hours, limit orders—at least in theory—are designed to expedite transactions as quickly as possible.

Other Mechanics of After-Hours Trading

To get a feel for other elements of extended hours trading, here are some guidelines offered at one online brokerage house:

▸ **Trading Hours**
Trades are accepted between 7:30 A.M. and 9:15 A.M. EST and between 4 P.M. and 8 P.M.

▸ **Order Placement**
Trades are accepted only via the brokerage house's website, unless the Internet is down.

▸ **Eligible Securities**
All listed and Nasdaq securities.

▸ **What Investors Are Allowed to Do**
Many ECNs are limited exclusively to limit orders (see sidebar).

▸ **What Investors Can't Do**
Short sales, stop limit, and stop loss sales.

▸ **Order Limitations**
Orders must be in multiples of 100 shares.

Advantages of After-Hours Trading

▸ **Equal Treatment.** Since institutions have been trading after hours for more than a decade, availability to individual investors further levels the playing field.

▸ **Price Movement.** Stocks do change in price after the markets have closed. After-hours trading lets investors take advantage of that movement.

▸ **News and Other Company Announcements.** Many companies prefer to wait until after the markets have closed to release news and make announcements—both positive and negative. Again, after-hours trading allows individual investors a means to access a stock when some news may be affecting its price after the markets have closed.

Drawbacks of After-Hours Trading

▸ **Bad Prices.** Since after-hours trading represents only a fraction of overall trading activity, that means there is less overall demand. This can make it more difficult for buyers to get a good price and, in turn, for sellers to get the sale price they might receive during the greater activity of normal trading hours. In fact, studies have shown that after-hours trading is consistently more costly to investors than trading during regular market hours.

▸ **Limited Choices.** Investors cannot do certain things—such as short a stock—that they can during conventional trading hours.

▸ **Overreaction.** Like day traders who buy and sell more often than they should, some financial pros are concerned that extended hours only further the temptation to tinker unnecessarily with investments. That can result in bad decisions and promote greater expense to investors.

▲ After-hours trading lets investors react faster to company news.

▼ After-hours trading is more expensive than regular market trading.

International Investing

International investing was touched on briefly in earlier sections. Here's a more detailed discussion of their pros and cons.

Overseas Stocks and Funds

Although they are a topic of some debate, there's something to be said for giving some thought to overseas stocks, bonds and mutual funds.

Why Invest Overseas

The traditional thinking has been that markets in other parts of the world don't necessarily move in sync with the American economy. Put another way, American companies which perform poorly don't necessarily adversely affect foreign companies. So, by investing in foreign stocks, you're achieving greater overall diversity than if you limited your choices to domestic companies.

Growth Potential

Another argument is that, compared with the United States, many countries with emerging markets have companies and industrial sectors that are just now starting to show promise of growth. By that reasoning, many have greater upside potential than domestic stocks.

The Unfortunate Truth

However, in recent years the above arguments haven't proven to be totally true. For one thing, when American markets have hit the skids, so, too, have other markets, such as in Europe. One reason is a move toward similar economies—with communication and trade practices becoming more global, overseas markets are developing in a fashion similar to the United States. They tend to react in the same way at the same time.

Again—Why Invest Overseas?

There's still something to be said for the diversity of overseas investments. For example, stocks from emerging economies—countries that are still developing economically—have occasionally outperformed domestic holdings. International proponents argue that diversifying overseas demands a long-term timeline to realize greater safety and profitability.

What to Consider in Foreign Stocks

▸ **Financial Information.** This has been a problem with some foreign stocks since accounting practices

Check the Hedge

Another issue to bear in mind is currency hedging. This is when fund managers sell foreign currencies to hedge the foreign security portfolio in case the currency drops against the dollar. Although it can work if the fund sells a currency that's going down in value, it can also backfire. If you're concerned about overall risk, ask whether a fund is involved in this sort of activity.

NOK Daily Average vs. DJIA

Change in Value

+30%
+20%
+10%
0%
-10%
-20%
-30%
-40%
-50%
-60%
-70%

Sep Oct Nov Dec 01 Feb Mar Apr May Jun Jul Aug

To illustrate the profit potential—as well as the volatility—of some overseas stocks, take a look at Finland-based Nokia. Over the course of a year, the cell phone giant easily outpaced the Dow Jones Industrials at times but, when faced with a slowdown in the economy, fell far below the Dow.

overseas differ. Look for what are called **American Depository Receipts** (ADRs), which represent shares in foreign companies that are traded on American exchanges. These have accounting and reporting practices similar to those followed by domestic companies.

▶ **Investment Expenses.** Although more brokerage houses offer international stocks than they used to, transaction costs can still be more expensive than buying domestic stock.

▶ **Currency Risk.** Since an overseas company is dealing in a different currency, valuation movement between that currency and the dollar can also affect the total return of the investment.

What to Consider in International Funds

▶ **Names.** International mutual funds come in all types. Some focus on one country, while others are more regionalized. Some specialize in small cap stocks. Check

the fund's holdings carefully (some, in fact, tout themselves as overseas funds but actually have a significant portion of their portfolios in American companies).

▶ **Make Sure of Diversity.** If you're investing overseas to diversify, make sure your overseas holdings don't simply mirror what you can buy domestically. For instance, some large cap overseas funds might move in the same way as large cap funds that own U.S. stock. That doesn't provide genuine diversification.

▶ **Cost.** Like individual stocks, many international mutual funds cost more since, the reasoning goes, it costs more to research overseas stocks than it does American companies.

▶ **Volatility.** The more specific a fund is, the greater the swing in its investment returns. If you're concerned about risk, make sure your fund diversifies (as opposed to funds that, for instance, may only invest in companies from one country).

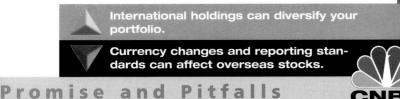

International holdings can diversify your portfolio.

Currency changes and reporting standards can affect overseas stocks.

Promise and Pitfalls

CNBC

Day Trading

Every other section in this book focuses largely on what you should do to better your chances for investing success. This section, by contrast, pays attention to something that you should likely avoid.

The Perils and Hollow Promise of Day Trading

With the advent of electronic investing, and the resulting immediacy and relative low cost of executing trades, day trading has become yet another strategy that some investors employ to try to profit from the stock market.

What It Is

In one sense, "day trading" is a misleading term, as it might suggest buying and holding stocks for at least 24 hours. That's often not the case—day traders move in and out of positions quickly, trying to capitalize on short-term price movements. Rather than buying a stock and keeping it for any length of time, day traders may hold stocks for only hours or even minutes.

How Many Day Traders Are There?

Although the issue has received a lot of press in recent years, federal estimates hold that there are only several thousand investors who trade enough on a daily basis to be classified as day traders.

Why Some People Think Day Trading Works

Given the immediate connection afforded by online trading systems, day traders think they have enough contact with the market to buy stocks over the short term and move out of them once they produce a profit. Day traders tend not to examine company fundamentals—rather, they're looking to ride a stock's short-term momentum and sell their holdings once that momentum has run its course. In other words, day traders emphasize technical analysis.

Why Day Trading Doesn't Work

The risks and drawbacks of day trading are numerous:

▸ **It Eliminates the Mitigating Effects of Time.** Since day traders are constantly moving in and out of positions, there's not enough time to reduce risk and volatility.

Firm Irregularities

Further evidence that day-trading firms are only interested in making a profit at the day trader's expense: A recent Senate study found that, not only did some firms encourage traders to open margin accounts to continue day trading, they occasionally helped clients set up accounts under fictitious names. This allowed them to continue trading if, for instance, they had lost other legitimate accounts because they couldn't meet margin calls.

Downside Numbers

For further evidence of the significant risks involved, here are some of the findings of a recent Senate investigation into day trading:

The study estimated that upwards of 15 percent of trading volume on the Nasdaq can be attributed to day-trading activity, even though the study speculated there are only several thousand active day traders.

The study said that the average day trader places close to 30 trades every day.

The average commission per trade was estimated at $16.

Given that commission average, the study calculated that the average day trader would have to make more than $480 every day just to break even.

Extrapolating that further, the bite of commissions means that the average day trader would have to make about $120,000 in stock profits annually just to break even.

Audits included as part of the Senate investigation found that 70 to 90 percent of day traders are unsuccessful and lose money as a result of day trading. Further, many day traders reportedly lose every penny they have.

▶ **Cost.** Even with decreases in commission structures (some brokers, in fact, cut special deals for day trading), making dozens of trades a day boosts the expense of investing. That makes profits even more difficult, even if a day trader is consistently picking winners.

▶ **Time Commitment.** Day traders have to watch the markets continually to try to adjust their holdings accordingly. This is virtually impossible if the investor has a job or some other commitment that can limit the amount of time spent monitoring the markets.

▶ **Firms That Specialize in Day Trading Aren't Necessarily on the Investor's Side.** Even though some brokerage houses cater to day traders by slashing commissions, they don't always act in investors' best interests.

A recent Senate study found that investor questionnaires—information supplied by investors to determine their emotional and financial suitability for day trading—were routinely ignored by day-trading houses.

The Senate study also found that day-trading houses commonly encouraged day traders to trade beyond their financial means, such as by opening margin accounts to underwrite day trading.

Day-trading sites also commonly provide clients with so-called "hot tips" and "expert advice," both of which often prove to be not in the least bit helpful.

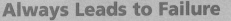

Day trading is an extremely risky activity that at times yields high returns.

Day trading runs counter to most reliable investing precepts.

Always Leads to Failure

Another Place to Find Help

Although it's natural to assume that investing and financial guidance must always come from a so-called "professional," that's by no means true. Thousands of investment clubs disprove that every day.

All About Investment Clubs

If the notion of a club geared to successful investing sounds appealing, here's a rundown on investment clubs, what they are, and why so many work as well as they do.

What They Are

The basic structure, which will differ from club to club depending on function and members' preferences, essentially involves a group of friends and associates getting together, establishing a set of bylaws and operating procedures, and pooling a preset amount of investment money together on a regular basis.

▶ **How Much Financial Commitment?** Again, that will differ, but clubs often mandate that members kick in $50 to $100 every month.

The Number of Clubs

The National Association of Investors Corporation (a group that provides information, education and other services on setting up and operating a successful club) claims more than 37,000 member clubs. Plus there are an untold number of other clubs outside of the NAIC.

How They Function

Again, this varies from club to club but, in general, clubs function in a democratic fashion to decide where to invest their common pool of funds. Members research stock, mutual funds, and other sorts of investments, then offer their recommendations to the group, which votes whether to invest and, if so, how much. Meeting on a regular basis, clubs track how their investments are performing, whether to make new investments or discard ones that are not performing up to par, and other such chores.

Online Clubs

Not all investment clubs are limited to face-to-face meetings. There are a few online investment clubs floating about in cyberspace, something that members say offers real advantages. While regular clubs are constrained by geography, an online investment club can recruit members from any part of the world. That can add diversity and a more global perspective to the group's operations, not to mention opening a club up to people whose schedule might not jibe with that of a live club. To check one out, have a look at the Coast-to-Coast Club (http://www.parlorcity.com/trump/CTCOLIC.htm).

Advantages

▶ **Necessary Legwork.** Unlike investing on your own, where you can occasionally jump into a stock or fund without truly doing your homework, investment clubs mandate that you make the case that a choice is a solid investment. Since a group is making the decision, that means becoming comfortable with everything from the annual report to keeping up-to-date on news and developments that can impact a stock or fund.

▶ **Education.** That, in turn, makes investment clubs a great source of investor education. Members learn how to read balance sheets, analysts' reports and other documents that are central to intelligent investing.

▶ **Autonomy.** Rather than relying on a stockbroker, planner, or some other financial pro hawking recommendations, investment clubs are proactive when it comes to charting their own investing strategy. This instills responsibil-ity and confidence instead of reliance on someone else.

▶ **The Social Aspect.** Many investors don't find the chores of researching and choosing stocks and funds to be particularly entertaining. By contrast, investment clubs instill a social element into investing (in fact, many investment clubs derive from other types of social gatherings, such as bridge clubs or groups of golfing buddies).

Where to Get More Information

If you're interested in finding out more about investment clubs, contact the National Association of Investors Corp. The NAIC provides extensive information about club creation and operations, including how to start a club, investing basics, software, club structures and bylaws, and frequently asked questions. Address: P.O. Box 220, Royal Oak, MI 48068 (website: www.better-investing.org).

Better Investing Top 100 Index

Period Ending 9/28/2001	BI Top 100	S&P 500	Dow Jones
Index Price	533.48	1,040.94	8,8497.56
Monthly Price Change	-8.1%	-8.2%	-11.1%
1 Year Total Return	-31.1%	-26.6%	-15.9%
3 Year Total Return	4.3%	2.0%	5.7%
5 Year Total Return	12.8%	10.2%	10.3%
10 Year Total Return	13.5%	12.7%	13.8%

Lest you think that investment clubs are for lightweights, compare the NAIC's Better Investing Top 100 Index versus the performance of other major indices. Their index comprises those companies most widely held by NAIC investment clubs. Calculated since 1986, the index is put together using surveys of NAIC-member clubs. To view this and more detailed information online, visit http://www.better-investing.org/content/top100index.html.

▲ Investment clubs are a great way to learn investing skills.

▼ Clubs are not a place for the lazy— you have to do your homework.

Commodities

Many of us are familiar with former First Lady—and now Senator—Hillary Clinton's profitable foray into the world of cattle futures. No matter what your political persuasion, Ms. Clinton's fast and substantial score illustrates the profit potential of commodities—a market and a form of investing that is every bit as risky as it can prove lucrative.

The Basics of Futures

Here's a rundown of some of the basic elements of commodities.

What They Are

Unlike stocks, commodities are raw materials, such as wheat, corn, soybeans, and other sorts of agricultural products as well as other items such as heating oil, gold, lumber and copper. Since these, like everything else, fluctuate in price depending on supply, demand, and other technical factors, the idea behind investing in commodities is to try to predict their future price movement.

Futures

▶ WHAT THEY ARE: Futures—or, more specifically, futures con-tracts—are a legally binding agreement to either buy or sell a specific quantity of a commodity in the future (as we'll note later, you can also buy futures contracts related to financial instruments like stock indices, bonds and currencies). Futures contracts can last less than a year or as long as several years. Futures trading takes place on exchanges throughout the world.

▶ WHAT THAT MEANS: When you buy a futures contract, you're effectively betting on the future price movement of a commodity. This is known as speculation.

Long. A long position means that you expect prices to increase.

Short. Just as the term implies with stock, a short position is taken in expectation of dropping prices.

▶ HOW FUTURES CONTRACTS WORK: An essential element of futures contracts is leverage. Leverage allows investors to purchase commodities contracts by only putting up a small portion of the actual value of the contract—usually anywhere from 5 to 10 percent of the overall value. For instance, if you want to buy a soybean futures contract that's worth $30,000, you might have to give a commodities broker only $3,000 (this is known as buying on margin).

▶ WHAT CAN GO RIGHT FROM THERE: Having bought into a futures contract at a fraction of its actual value—you've taken a long position—any increase in the value

Risk Check

Since investing in commodities is remarkably risky—estimates hold that more than three-quarters of all newcomers lose money—many brokerage houses require stringent checks before setting up an account. They're supposed to ask about your experience, income, assets and other factors to see if you're in a position to invest in commodities (and, quite possibly, take a bath in the process).

of the commodity gives you a profit. For example, if the value of soybeans goes up 25 percent, that represents a profit of $7,500, more than double the amount of money you actually had to put up. This illustrates the power of leverage.

▶ WHAT CAN GO WRONG: Unfortunately, the opposite can be true (and frequently is). Should the price of soybeans go down, an investor's losses are also magnified as well. For instance, if soybeans drop 5 percent in value, that's a loss of $1,500. Even worse, if soybeans fall 10 percent, that's a $3,000 loss—your entire initial investment is gone.

▶ EVEN WORSE: Should the price of the commodity plunge below what you put up as an investment, you'll receive a margin call from your broker asking you for cash to make up the difference.

▶ BOTTOM LINE: With futures

you can make a quick profit many times over your investment or actually lose more money than you put up in the first place.

Getting Out of a Futures Contract

Don't worry about barrels of oil suddenly appearing on your lawn—that won't happen if you close out your position before the delivery date. Only a tiny fraction of futures contracts actually live out their full lifespan. Instead, most investors settle their positions by buying or selling a contract that represents the opposite position of the original contract. (For instance, you can get out of a contract to buy soybeans by selling a soybean contract. That cancels the obligation to buy and you pocket the profit or take your losses.)

Imagine the Possibilities

To illustrate the inherent rewards and risks of futures contracts, consider the following investment scenario.

Step One: An investor takes a long position with a wheat contract worth $50,000. That involves 10,000 bushels at $5 a bushel.

Step Two: To take a position requires a 10 percent investment, or $5,000.

Step Three: Summer storms devastate the Midwest, dropping wheat supplies and increasing the value of existing stores. The price goes up $1.50 a bushel.

Step Four: The investor could then sell a wheat contract to liquidate his position. Profit: $15,000, less commissions and other expenses—three times his initial investment.

Here's a variation on the above scenario.

Step Three: The Midwest has an ideal wheat production season, dropping the value of wheat per bushel some 75 cents.

Step Four: Should he liquidate his position, that would result in a $7,500 loss.

Step Five: Not only does he lose his entire $5,000 investment, the investor also has to make good on the additional $2,500 lost through the contract by meeting a margin call.

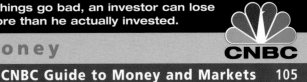

Futures can make fast profits through leverage.

If things go bad, an investor can lose more than he actually invested.

Commodities and Options

While futures are an undeniably risky way to get into the commodities market, options offer an alternative means that's not quite so chancy.

Commodities and the Basics of Options

Here's an overview of options and how they function somewhat differently from futures.

What They Are

Unlike a futures contract, which involves the legal commitment to buy or sell something, an option is less constricting. Instead, an option gives the investor the right—but not the obligation—to buy or sell a futures contract. Within options are two primary variations:

▸ **Calls.** These represent the right to buy a futures contract. An investor would do this on expectation that the commodity is going to increase in price.

▸ **Puts.** These give the right to sell a futures contract. By contrast, investors use puts when they expect prices to drop.

HELPFUL HINT: To keep the two terms straight, remember the terms "call up" and "put down," so you know which one applies to a particular type of price movement.

Other Terms to Remember

▸ **Premium.** As is the case with buying insurance, this is the price an investor pays to buy options.

▸ **Strike Price.** This refers to the specific price that an option gives an investor to buy a contract (for calls) or to sell the contract (when using puts). Options usually last no longer than a year. Also known as the exercise price.

How Options Can Work

Options give investors the right to purchase certain contracts within a specified time frame. Investors buying calls are hoping that the contract will rise in value, while investors with puts are pulling for prices to drop.

Like futures, options offer investors leverage, meaning that the size of the contract involved is worth many times over the amount of money an investor is actually putting up. For instance, an investor may buy a gold options contract controlling $50,000 worth of gold for as little as $2,500 (5 percent of the actual value of the contract).

Derivatives

Both futures and options are known by the term "derivatives." This is because, unlike a stock which has value unto itself, futures and options' values derive from something else. The underlying asset may be a commodity, stock index or bond.

Price Movements

Here's an illustration of how price movement can affect the profitability—or lack thereof—in one call-option contract.

Step One: An investor buys a call option with a strike price of $20 on 1,000 barrels of crude oil for $700.

Step Two: If the price stays at or below the $20 strike price...
Value at contract expiration: $0
Loss: $700

Step Three: If the crude oil price moves up $1 above the $20 strike price to $21 per barrel...
Value at contract expiration: $1,000
Profit: $300

Step Four: If the crude oil price moves up $2 above the $20 strike price to $22 per barrel...
Value at contract expiration: $2,000
Profit: $1,300

Step Five: If the crude oil price moves up $3 above the $20 strike price to $23 per barrel...
Value at contract expiration: $3,000
Profit: $2,300

Step Six: If the crude oil price moves up $5 above the $20 strike price to $25 per barrel...
Value at contract expiration: $5,000
Profit: $4,300

Note: This exercise also illustrates that, given the expense of the premium, the value of a contract must sufficiently exceed the strike price to offset the premium if the investor is to earn a profit.

The Mechanics of Options

Options follow a course that's largely similar to futures. Call players want the price to go up, while investors with puts want the price to drop (read: every bit as unpredictable as futures contracts' price movement). The difference is the downside—while, with futures, you can end up losing more than the money you actually invested, with options all you can lose is the money you invested, since they involve only the rights but not the obligations to buy or sell.

EXAMPLE: If you buy call options on a futures contract for 5,000 bushels of corn at $5 a bushel, say the strike price is $6.50 and the contract expires in six months. If the price rises to $7 a bushel, the investor who sold you that contract (known as the investor who wrote the call) is obligated to sell you bushels of corn worth $7 a bushel for only $6.50. That's a $2,500 profit, minus the premium you paid to buy the contract.

By contrast, if the price of the bushels never exceeds the strike price, an investor merely lets the contract expire; all he's out is the price of the premium.

The same holds true with puts. Should the price drop below the strike price, you're in the money. If it doesn't, your premium is gone when the contract expires.

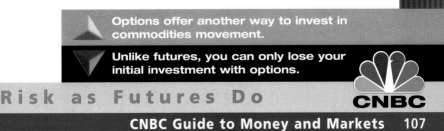

Options offer another way to invest in commodities movement.

Unlike futures, you can only lose your initial investment with options.

Risk as Futures Do

CNBC

More on Commodities

Other than the techniques described in the prior two sections, there are other ways to use futures and options. Unlike a purely speculative approach, however, these strategies may actually help investors hedge or limit risk associated with their existing investment.

Other Ways to Use Futures and Options

A commonly used term—both on CNBC television and at CNBC.com—is "futures." Specifically, stock index futures connected with the Dow Jones Industrial Average, the Nasdaq, and the S&P 500.

What They Are

Stock index futures—like any other type of future—involve a contract to deliver something at a specific date for a set price. In this case—unlike other futures, where the underlying value of the con-tract comes from something like wheat or oil—the underlying value is a stock index.

How They Work

One way to use stock index futures effectively is to protect a stock port-folio from unnecessary risk. Here's an example—if an investor owns a large number of S&P 500 stocks and has enjoyed significant gains from those holdings, she may be con-cerned that they'll go down in value, cutting into her overall profit.

How Stock Futures Can Help

Stock index futures, for the most part, follow the lead of the actual stock index—when it goes up, so do they and vice versa. If an investor is worried about dropping S&P 500 stock prices, she might consider shorting an S&P 500 futures contract.

▶ Advantages: If the investor guesses right and stock prices do go down, so likely will the stock futures contract. Although the investor will have lost money from the drop in stock prices, it's offset somewhat by profits from the futures contract.

▶ Disadvantages: Obviously, if the opposite happens, whatever additional profits realized by the

Serious Risk

Commodities are a very risky way to invest, par-ticularly when compared with stocks, mutual funds and other more conservative investi-ments. Not only can you lose because of a poorly timed investment, but commodities can also be negatively effected by such things as weather and political decisions. That's a slice of reality that can burn profes-sionals, let alone the rel-atively inexperienced.

investor's stock holdings will be diminished by losses from the futures contract. Add to that the expense of buying the futures contract.

Using Options

Like index futures, an investor can also use options in a number of ways.

▶ **Buying a Protective Put.** This involves buying an option connected with a specific stock. Again, it can also be used as a means to protect against unwanted price movement with the stock itself. For instance, if an investor is concerned that a stock's price is going to go down, he can hedge his position by buying a put option. This lets the investor earn some offsetting profit if the stock's price does, in fact, go down. Alternatively, an investor could sell, or "write" a call against a stock he owns. While offering no protection against loss, this does create income to the investor in the amount of the premium, which in effect offsets part of the loss.

▶ **Naked Options.** Here, an investor is employing options without actually owning the stock. This is a very risky play equivalent to options on commodity futures. While covered options offer some sort of hedge by actually owning the stock, naked options can burn investors if the price of the stock moves in the wrong direction. That's a pure loss with nothing to help offset it.

Terms of the Trade

Here's a glossary of other terms associated with futures and options:

Arbitrage. This is a way to profit when the same security is traded on more than one market. In essence, an investor buys whatever's less expensive and sells the more expensive at the same time, betting on the difference between the two securities.

At the Money. When the strike price is the same as the underlying asset price.

In the Money. A call option is in-the-money if the strike price is less than the market price of the underlying security. A put option is in-the-money if the strike price is greater than the market price of the underlying security.

Out of the Money. A call option is out-of-the-money if the strike price is greater than the market price of the underlying security. A put option is out-of-the-money if the strike price is less than the market price of the underlying security.

Straddling. This means an investor buys a call and a put on the same underlying investment. This is designed to produce a profit no matter which way the investment's price moves. The strike price of both is the same.

▲ Options and futures can be used to protect stock holdings.

▼ Things can still go wrong if the price moves unexpectedly.

More Potential, More Risk

CNBC

Budgeting Investment Goals

Before any of us can get down to mapping out a winning investment strategy, it's essential to have certain aspects of your money life in line first. The next several sections will address ways you can find money to invest, strategies to protect what you've earned and smart moves to get the most out of your money.

Setting Up A Budget

Establishing and following a budget isn't going to make anyone's top-ten list of earthly delights. Nonetheless, setting up and sticking to a workable budget is an essential element of your financial well-being, and it doesn't have to be an act of self-torture. Here are a few suggestions and guidelines for building a budget that you can live with.

Start by Tracking Your Spending

Rather than imposing abstract budgetary guidelines—20 percent for housing, 20 percent for food, etc.—track your spending for a couple of months to see where your money is going. Follow everything as closely as possible. Chances are good that this simple exercise alone may target places where unnecessary cash is being spent.

Then, Set Up a Budget Accordingly

Once you've got a handle on your spending habits and know where you can shore things up, set up your budget following those general guidelines. For example, you may not be able to do much about your mortgage or rent (unless, of course, you can refinance your mortgage) but look to other areas if you'd like to save some money. For instance, trimming your weekly grocery bill by a mere $25 frees up $100 a month for investing. Look into raising insurance deductibles, which, in turn, may lower your premiums.

Prorate Major Expenses

One of the biggest problems with many budgets is that they ignore significant expenses that don't come up all that often—say, insur-

Focus on the Goal

One way to become comfortable with a budget has to do with attitude. Instead of seeing a budget as a financial constraint, treat it as an opportunity to save money for important goals—retirement, housing, significant purchases, and other desirable things. Treating your budget as a financial ally rather than an enemy can make it easier to follow.

Developing a Workable Budget Can

Choose to Save

If you think cutting back on your spending can't make a real difference to your long-term financial well-being, have a look at some of these scenarios. To get an idea of how much you actually might save, plug in your own numbers and work them through the various time frames:

Choosing to buy a less expensive car	**Monthly savings: $150** **Annual savings: $1,800** **Savings over ten years: $22,161**
Paying off credit cards monthly instead of carrying a balance	**Monthly savings: $200** **Annual savings: $2,400** **Savings over ten years: $29,548**
Going to fewer movies	**Monthly savings: $30** **Annual savings: $600** **Savings over the years: $7,387**
<u>**Totals from these three items**</u>	**Monthly savings: $380** **Annual savings: $4,600** **Savings over ten years: $56,141**

ance premiums that only come due every six months. To avoid having these costs sneak up on you, prorate them on a monthly basis—if your car insurance is payable every six months, cut a check every month for one-sixth the amount and put the money in a money market fund. Do the same sort of thing with more enjoyable expenses. If you want to take a vacation in a year's time and have a reasonably good idea how much it might cost, divvy up the expense by 12 and set it aside on a monthly basis.

Other Budget Savers

Here are a few additional ideas and strategies that will help you to set up and stick with a livable budget:

▸ **Keep an eye on ATM activity.** Automatic cash machines can be downright insidious. All too often, it's hard to track just how often we hit them up for

cash. Hard it may be, but do your utmost not to let ATM visits get away from you. One way is to carry your checkbook everywhere you go and record an ATM withdrawal on the spot.

▸ **Pay with cash.** This may seem to contradict the prior item, but one way to keep a handle on your spending is to pay with cash whenever you can. It's a simple dynamic—rather than racking up charges on a credit card without knowing just how much those charges are amounting to, paying with cash imposes a built-in discipline. If you don't have it, you can't spend it.

▸ **Consider a debit card.** This will be covered in greater detail in the credit card section, but using a debit card—one that automatically removes cash from an account when it's used—can also be a real budget saver. Not only do you save on interest charges, but you can only use money that you have.

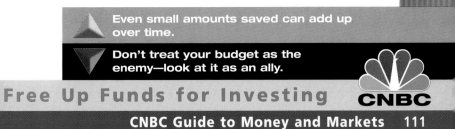

Even small amounts saved can add up over time.

Don't treat your budget as the enemy—look at it as an ally.

Digging Out of Credit Card Debt

One obstacle to freeing up funds for investing is, ironically, a symbol of affluence for many people. Credit card debt is a burden and digging your way out is another important step in securing overall financial health.

Ways to Pare Down and Manage Credit Card Debt

Americans owe more than $500 billion in credit card debt. That statistic alone suggests the scope of the problem of credit card debt and, in turn, how much it can affect positive financial habits such as a systematic program of investing and saving. Fortunately, getting your credit cards under control is not an impossibility. Consider some of the following steps:

▶ **First, add up what you owe.** It may be surprising, but people with a number of credit cards may not be aware of the actual size of their debt. Don't be one of them—gather every card you have and tally up the balances.

▶ **Cut up extra cards.** There's really no reason to carry more than two or, at most, three credit cards. If you have more than that, cut up the extras and call the issuers to close the accounts. In particular, target cards with high interest rates.

▶ **Consolidate balances.** Once you've closed out high rate cards, transfer those balances to cards with lower interest rates. Give some thought to moving the balances into a teaser credit card with an exceedingly low interest rate. These are cards that levy little or no interest but whose rates spike up after a period of time. If you do transfer balances to teaser cards, be sure to set up an aggressive payment plan to pay down the balance before the interest rate jumps.

▶ **Pay more than the minimum.** Whether you opt for a teaser card or consolidate balances into cards you already have, figure out how much more above the minimum monthly payment you can afford. This is perhaps the most critical step in paring down credit card debt—by adding money beyond the monthly minimum, you're

Paying It Down

Got several cards with differing balances? There are a couple of ways to tackle a paydown program. If you want to eliminate the big ones first, target extra payments to those cards with the largest balances. On the other hand, some people feel better about eliminating the smaller ones quickly. For many, that feels like they're moving toward their eventual goal faster.

Controlling Credit Card Debt Can

effectively paying down what you owe rather than simply paying interest. That reduces the amount of money you actually owe on the cards.

▶ **Consider a home equity line of credit.** Homeowners may also give some thought to taking out a line of credit to pay off outstanding credit card balances. Home equity lines offer two distinct advantages—first, their interest rates are almost always lower than many credit cards. Second, interest—unlike that from credit cards—is tax deductible.

▶ **Tap into savings.** One final option to reduce credit card debt is to use savings to pay off outstanding balances. On the surface, this may seem like the least appealing choice, but it is a viable option if you're serious about getting out from credit card debt. Look at it this way—if your savings are in a money market fund earning 5 percent and you pay off credit cards with an average interest rate of 11 percent, that's an effective 6 percent return on your money.

How to Save

Not all credit card problems are due to staggering balances. It also pays to watch for fees, charges, and other costs associated with certain cards. Here's a rundown of shopping tips to keep these expenses under control:

Consider paying for a lower rate card. Some cards impose an annual fee which, in turn, gives the holder a lower interest rate. For some people—particularly those who use their cards a lot and usually carry a balance—it makes sense. However, if you don't carry a balance or don't use the card all that much, avoid annual fees. They're a wasted expense.

Get a card where you bank. Check whether your bank offers any sort of special deal—in some cases, account holders get better deals than those offered by credit card companies. If nothing's advertised, ask anyway—there's always the chance that you can get a good deal if the bank wants to keep your business.

Shop aggressively. Credit cards are fighting like mad for your business. Shop around to secure the best possible card that you can, both in terms of the interest rate as well as any sort of other charges and fees that may be attached to the card.

Consider a debit card. Debit cards can be a cost-effective alternative to conventional credit cards. If nothing else, you save on interest rates since funds are removed from an account every time you use the card—that can also short-circuit the types of spending binges that can come with a regular credit card. One caveat—since the money's automatically withdrawn, it's generally more difficult to challenge a bill with a debit card.

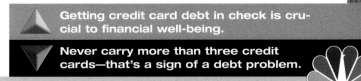

▲ Getting credit card debt in check is crucial to financial well-being.

▼ Never carry more than three credit cards—that's a sign of a debt problem.

Mean Significant Savings

Buying a Home

Few financial commitments in life carry more import than buying a home. For many people, it represents the single largest financial transaction they'll ever pursue. So, it's important to know a few strategies to ensure that you get the best home deal you possibly can.

The Financial Considerations

Many aspects of home buying— choosing a neighborhood, the type of home, and other considerations—are too mercurial to address. However, many of the financial mechanics associated with purchasing a home apply to most home buyers:

▸ **The Down Payment.** Headache number one for the lion's share of home buyers. Banks and other lenders typically expect you to put down 5 to 20 percent of the home's purchase price. On top of that you must add on closing costs, attor-

ney's fees, and other expenses that usually amount to another 5 percent of the purchase price.

Ways to Amass A Down Payment

▸ **Loans** from family or friends.

▸ **Programs** such as the Federal Housing Administration, the Veterans Administration and other national programs that require less than a 20 percent down payment.

▸ **Withdrawals from an IRA** (for first-time home buyers only—see the section on IRAs for more details). Also borrowing from a 401k plan where you work.

▸ **Private mortgage insurance** (PMI). Imposes a monthly premium until equity in the home reaches 20 percent. Recent legislative changes make it easier for home buyers to eliminate PMI once their home equity reaches the necessary 20 percent level.

▸ CONTACT INFORMATION. The FHA website is http://www.hud.gov/offices/hsg/index.cfm. Call (202) 708-1112.

The VA website is http://www.va.gov/. Call (800) 827-1000.

How Much Home Can You Afford

This, like other elements of home buying, can vary. But the follow-

---

Points?

To point or not to point— that's the question for many homebuyers. Points— upfront charges prorated based on the size of a home loan—can reduce a mortgage's interest rate. The easiest way to determine whether you should pay points or not depends on how long you think you'll stay in the home—in general, the shorter your expected stay, the less the rationale for points, since you won't be in the house long enough to make up the expense through interest payment savings.

Adding Extra to Mortgage Payments Cuts

Paying Down Your Mortgage Faster

Like credit cards, it's often a great idea to tack on extra to your mortgage payment. Again, by doing so you're tackling the principal amount owed rather than just interest charges. If you think even a small amount added on can't make a difference, check out the following scenarios:

Size of mortgage	$100,000
Interest rate	7.5 percent
Length of mortgage	30 years
Basic monthly payment	$699.21
Extra monthly payment	$100
Total interest with extra $100 payment	$95,405
Total interest without extra payment	$151,717
Interest saved	$56,312

Mortgage paid off in approximately 20 years

The difference becomes even greater the larger the mortgage:

Size of mortgage	$200,000
Interest rate	7.5 percent
Length of mortgage	30 years
Basic monthly payment	$1,398
Extra monthly payment	$100
Total interest with extra $100 payment	$232,178
Total interest without extra payment	$303,434
Interest saved	$91,256

Mortgage paid off in approximately 24 years

To see the savings on a specific loan, have a look at the "calculators" section at the Bankrate Monitor (www.bankrate.com).

ing, among others, are some commonly suggested guidelines:

▸ Home price should not exceed 2½ times household gross income.

▸ Monthly mortgage payments—including insurance and property taxes—should not be greater than 28 percent of household gross income.

▸ Monthly housing expenses, along with other long-term debts such as credit card payments and alimony, should not exceed 36 percent of gross household income.

What Sort of Mortgage

Although mortgages come with all sorts of wrinkles and variables, for many home buyers the question boils down to choosing between a fixed rate mortgage or an adjustable loan whose interest rate will change over time. Although a definitive answer can depend on all sorts of financial considerations, the simple answer has to do with time frame—the shorter the amount of time you expect to stay in a home, the more compelling the argument for an adjustable rate mortgage whose interest rate is lower than its fixed counterpart.

There are a variety of ways to come up with a home purchase down payment.

Avoid paying points if you expect to stay in a home for a short time.

Saving for College

Saving for a college education—possibly one of your most significant long-term goals—can entail some very specific strategies.

College Savings Strategies

With the cost of college continuing to skyrocket—as of this writing, estimates put four years at a state university at about $80,000 or so, and at $160,000 for a private institution—it pays to know the various ways you can tackle this expense.

Different Ways to Save

UNIFORM GIFT TO MINORS ACCOUNTS (UGMAs)

HOW IT WORKS: Under current law, UGMAs let adults give minors up to $10,000 a year. The adult acts as the custodian of the account and selects how the money is invested.

ADVANTAGES: Since the account is technically owned by the minor, it's taxed at his or her rate—likely to be less than what an adult would pay in taxes.

DRAWBACKS: Once the minor reaches 18 years old (in some states, 21), the money becomes his to do with as he wishes. The young person may also lose out on financial aid should the money actually go toward college funding. Under current funding guidelines, money in the child's name counts for more than funds coming from someone else, reducing the amount of aid he or she may be eligible to receive.

UNIFORM TRANSFER TO MINORS (UTMA)

HOW IT WORKS: UTMAs are similar to UGMA accounts. The biggest difference is that UTMAs allow a greater variety of investments in the account than UGMAs, including partnerships and vehicles other than stocks and bonds.

ADVANTAGES AND DRAWBACKS: Like UGMAs, there are some tax advantages, but the drawback is that the coming-of-age minor can do with the money as he wishes. It can also be problematic when applying for financial aid.

529 COLLEGE SAVINGS PLAN

HOW IT WORKS: Managed by states, 529 plans let adults earmark large upfront contributions for col-

Pay to Prepay?

Another funding option is known as a prepaid tuition program. With this a parent gives money to a state funding program that allows a lock-in of current tuition rates. This plan, however, has some drawbacks—the biggest being limited choice. In many cases, a prepaid tuition program only covers a certain number of schools. If the child wants to go elsewhere or forgoes college completely, some programs offer very limited refund choices. And, like other types of funding schemes, prepaid tuition programs are in the child's name, which may hurt other sources of financial aid.

UGMAs, 529 Plans, and Others Offer

Strategy Guide

Here's a quick summary of the advantages and drawbacks of various types of college funding strategies.

Parents Investing Money
Advantages: Complete control over money; no limitations as to how much can be saved.
Drawbacks: No tax advantages; accounts are taxed as regular income.

Education IRAs
Advantages: Parent retains control over the account; tax-free qualified withdrawals usable for grades K–12.
Drawbacks: Limited to $2,000 per year in contribution; also harms chances for financial aid.

529 Plans
Advantages: Generous contribution amounts; federal income tax-free qualified withdrawals; adult retains ownership of the plan.
Drawback: Loss of control over how money is invested.

UGMA or UTMAs
Advantages: Contributions up to $10,000 a year allowed; gains are taxed at child's rate.
Drawbacks: Child actually owns the fund, which means funds may go to something other than college. Also, harmful to chances for receiving financial aid.

Prepaid Tuition Plans
Advantage: Allows participants to lock in current tuition rates.
Drawbacks: Limits the number of schools a child may attend and still qualify for the tuition plan; some refund programs are rather cheap in what they'll return if the child doesn't use the program.

lege—up to $250,000, depending on the individual state plan.

ADVANTAGES: There are several. For one thing, much larger deposit levels when compared with other programs. Also, as of 2002, newly signed legislation allows beneficiaries to avoid federal taxes when withdrawing funds for qualifying college costs. 529 College Savings Plans also offer a generous lifetime gift tax exemption for contributions. Additionally, the adult owns the plan—that means no problems once the money is withdrawn as well as less impact on financial-aid funding. Finally, under newly adopted guidelines, plan participants may roll over accounts from one state's 529 plan to another state's as often as once a year without any sort of tax or penalty.

DRAWBACKS: Unless the new tax law is extended, this particular tax treatment of withdrawals will end in December 2010. Taking part in a 529 plan ostensibly turns investment decisions over to officials overseeing a particular state's programs. Returns from individual states vary, so it's important to compare.

NOTE: Another funding option is an Education IRA. This is covered in the section entitled "Other Types of IRAs."

There are a number of options to fund a college education.

Start soon—college costs will continue to skyrocket.

Life Insurance

A central element of financial strength is protecting your wealth. The next several sections discuss various types of insurance, the kinds you may or may not need as well as how they can fit into an overall financial program.

Choosing Life Insurance

For many people, life insurance is an absolute must. In its most basic form, life insurance is used to replace income in the event of the policy holder's death. But for many others, life insurance is a consummate waste of money.

Do You Need Life Insurance?

This question has spawned more "creative" answers than you would care to hear, but there's a simple way to cut to the truth. If there is no one—a spouse, child, or parent—whose well-being depends on the income you produce, then there's no need for life insurance. Put another way, if there's no one around depending on your livelihood, then who are you protecting with the insurance?

Types of Life Insurance

However, if you do have someone relying on your income, then give life insurance some serious consideration. Here's a rundown of some of the major types of insurance you're likely to hear about:

▶ **Term.** This is the most basic form of protection. You pay the premium, and the insurance is in place for a certain amount of time. There is no savings element, as there is with other types of insurance.

ADVANTAGES: This is the best choice for many. It's usually the least expensive.

DRAWBACKS: Premiums generally increase as the policy holder gets older.

WRINKLES: Level term insurance,

in which the premium remains the same for several years. Also decreasing term, under which the premium remains the same but the policy's death benefit decreases.

▶ **Whole Life.** This type of insurance also includes a savings component. In that sense, what you're paying in premiums covers both the insurance itself as well as building a cash value for the policy.

ADVANTAGES: If you find it hard to save money, the cash element of term can be advantageous. Also, earnings from whole life insurance are tax-free.

DRAWBACKS: There are several. The most noteworthy: whole life is more expensive than term, particularly in the early years of the policy when much of what you're paying goes toward sales commissions. Another drawback—should you

An Investment?

Should life insurance be treated as a form of investing? That issue has raged for years with no definitive answer yet in sight. Although, as covered above, certain policies do offer a cash element, it's often best to focus on insurance's core function—protection. Pay the most attention to that—along with the affordability of the coverage you choose—and treat any sort of cash value as an ancillary benefit.

cash out the policy early, you pay a surrender charge which reduces the amount of money you receive.

Other Types of Cash Value Insurance.

▶ **Universal Life Insurance.** This is a rather flexible form of whole life insurance. Within certain parameters, the policy holder can choose how large a premium to pay. Policies also let you adjust the size of both the death benefit as well as the cash value of the policy.

▶ **Variable Life Insurance.** This type of insurance lets the policy holder decide how to invest the policy's cash element. Choices can include stocks, bonds and other investments.

▶ **Second-to-Die Insurance.** This policy effectively insures two people. No benefit is paid when the first person dies—the death benefit is only paid after the second person passes away.

Calculating the Death Benefit

Other than the type of policy you choose, the other essential decision pertaining to life insurance is the size of the death benefit. This is every bit as important as the form of coverage—not only does the size of the death benefit affect how much you pay in premiums, but it's essential that you obtain sufficient coverage. To help estimate that, use the following worksheet.

Step One: Add up the annual living expenses for the people protected by the life insurance. Multiply by the number of years the life insurance will be in force (to be particularly complete, you may want to adjust some of the later years to account for inflation).

Total Amount _____

Step Two: Add on any additional costs. These can include college expenses, emergency costs, funeral expenses, or a nest egg for the people protected by the insurance.

Total Amount _____

Amount from Steps One and Two: _____

Step Three: Calculate any income from any person covered by the insurance (it's best to use after-tax income). Again, multiply annual income by the number of years the insurance is in place.

Total Amount: _____

Step Four: Calculate any annual income from investments times the number of years the insurance is in force.

Total Amount: _____

Step Five: Calculate income from Social Security (call a local branch for more information).

Total Amount: _____

Step Six: Add up Steps Three through Five.

Amount from Steps Three through Five: _____

Step Seven: Subtract total from Step Six from total from Step Two.

Step Two minus Step Six: _____

This gives a reasonable estimate of your life insurance needs.

▲ Life insurance can help protect your loved ones' financial needs.

▼ Don't buy life insurance if there's no one who needs protection.

Health Insurance

Health insurance is essential for everyone. Here's a rundown of how to make certain you are adequately protected.

Coverage Options

Though the options can be bewildering, health insurance coverage really boils down to a few general choices. Which one you choose depends on your needs and how much you want to spend.

Coverage Through Your Employer

Needless to say, this is the easiest and most attractive of the choices for many people. Many companies—including those with relatively few employees—provide health coverage through some sort of group program. Take advantage of it—compared with getting insurance on your own, the coverage is inexpensive. Premiums are automatically deducted from your paycheck.

Finding It on Your Own

Unfortunately, some companies don't offer health insurance cover-age. Moreover, if you're self-employed, it's incumbent upon you to track down health insurance. Health insurance—for the most part—comes in three major categories and is offered through three primary sources:

▶ **Basic Insurance.** This is the plain vanilla of health insurance. You're usually covered for certain expenses up to a certain amount—that includes hospitalization.

▶ **Comprehensive Insurance.** This, like the name implies, is thorough medical coverage, including physical exams and other sorts of services bypassed by other coverage. This is generally the most expensive option.

▶ **Major Medical.** This is generally used to cover only significant medical expenses, such as surgery and hospitalization. Deductibles can be substantial. The good news is that this is often the least expensive form of coverage.

The Programs

▶ **Fee for Service Plan.** Of the three choices, this option has been around the longest. It's rather simple—you generally have to meet a deductible before the insurance coverage kicks in and there's usually a form of co-pay thereafter—about 20 percent. However, once your expenses hit a certain amount, the co-pay is eliminated and the insurer pays everything from there on.

Do You Belong?

Some fraternal organizations and alumni associations provide health insurance to their members. Likewise, check with any sort of business or professional group that you belong to—these also often offer health insurance that's less expensive than coverage you have to buy on your own.

ADVANTAGES: Complete freedom of choice. Unlike other options, you choose your doctor and make pretty much every other decision about what medical services you want and who will provide it.

DISADVANTAGES: Increasingly expensive as insurers make policy holders pick up a growing array of costs. Also, since the policy works as a form of reimbursement, you can end up waiting months for your insurance company to send you a check.

▶ **Health Maintenance Organization (HMOs).** With this option, you pay a premium and then a small fee every time you use the HMO for some sort of health service.

ADVANTAGES: Can prove the least expensive of all three options, particularly if you encounter a hefty bill such as an extended hospital stay.

DISADVANTAGES: The most limiting of the three choices. The plan specifies participating doctors and hospitals—stray from that list and your care becomes much more expensive. Also, getting referrals to specialists and other sorts of supplementary care can often be difficult.

▶ **Preferred Provider Organizations (PPOs).** Here, a policy holder is given a choice of doctors and other health care providers from which she can choose. If you use one of them, your costs are relatively low—usually a modest co-payment. However, if you use someone not on the list, your costs are significantly larger.

ADVANTAGES: Greater range of choice than HMOs offer.

DISADVANTAGES: Still limiting in some cases. If you join a PPO and you want to stick with a doctor you've been seeing for years, your costs can still be substantial if your physician isn't on the PPO's list of preferred providers.

The MSA Solution

Another option available to small businesses and the self-employed is a Medical Savings Account. Here's how it works and how it may be able to cut your coverage costs:

The first step is to sign up for high deductible health insurance:

Sample Deductible	$4,500 for a family, $2,250 for an individual.
Sample Family Premium	$400 a month, versus $700 for a more comprehensive plan.

Medical Savings Accounts let you deposit 75 percent of a family's deductible—or 65 percent of an individual's deductible—into a tax-free savings account.

For a $4,500 family deductible	$3,375 maximum yearly deposit.
For a $2,250 individual deductible	$1,462 maximum yearly deposit.

MSA contributions are fully tax deductible and the funds can be used to pay for qualified expenses before you reach the policy's deductible. If you don't use the money in an MSA, the money continues to earn tax-free interest similar to an IRA.

▲ Options such as medical savings accounts can cut health coverage expenses.

▼ No matter what you choose, never go without health insurance.

That's Not Optional

Homeowner's Insurance

Although mortgage lenders require any homebuyer to have homeowner's insurance, it still pays to understand how such policies work and how to choose one that provides adequate coverage in a cost-effective manner.

What Is It, What You Get

Here's the rundown on precisely what to shop for.

The Components of Homeowner's Insurance

▶ **Homeowner's insurance performs two primary functions.** First and foremost, it protects your home as well as your possessions. That means coverage against everything from a fire to a burglar who breaks in and makes off with your valuables. In addition, homeowner's insurance also affords liability coverage in the event that something of a potentially litigious nature occurs—say, the mailman is bitten by your dog and takes you to court.

▶ **The First Rule of Homeowner's Insurance.** Never cut corners with the protective element of your homeowner's coverage—the potential losses from inadequate coverage can be staggering:

Dwelling Coverage. This is the amount of coverage that's specific to the structure of the house itself. It's essential that you obtain enough coverage to ensure that your home would be completely rebuilt in the event it was destroyed by fire. So, don't underestimate the actual value of your home.

Guaranteed Replacement Coverage. Since it's often difficult to determine precisely how much money it might take to replace a home, this is the easiest way to make certain that your home is completely covered. This means that your insurance company guarantees to cover the cost of rebuilding your home, regardless of the cost.

Guaranteed Replacement Coverage for Possessions. The same rule of thumb should apply to your possessions. Rather than trying to estimate how much any particular possession might be worth, obtain guaranteed replacement coverage.

▶ **Liability Insurance.** This second element of homeowner's insurance—as discussed above—provides protection from personal injury and other similar occurrences. One rule of thumb is to obtain enough liability insurance to cover the value of your assets. In general, a good homeowner's policy

Make a Record

One tip that may provide a more complete form of homeowner's insurance is to make a videotape of your home. Go from room to room, taping valuables and particularly interesting or unusual architectural features of your home. That way, should something occur, you have a visual record that may expedite adequate insurance coverage.

will provide at least $300,000 of liability coverage.

Other Issues to Consider with Homeowner's Insurance

Don't make the mistake of assuming that an everyday homeowner's policy is naturally all-inclusive. In particular, two areas of potential coverage warrant attention:

▶ **Flood Insurance.** Basic homeowner's insurance generally doesn't include flood protection, but there's a very good chance you might need it. Ask whether your local government takes part in the federal National Flood Insurance System. If they do, contact the flood insurance program at (800) 638-6620. Your insurance agent may also be able to provide you with a map that delineates areas of flood risk. That, too, can tell you whether you need to obtain flood insurance.

▶ **Earthquake Insurance.** You may be surprised to find that your part of the country is more vulnerable than you might have thought. In particular, if where you live has any sort of history with earthquakes, ask about adding on earthquake insurance. Like flood insurance, this is a form of protection that many vanilla-type homeowner's policies do not address.

How to Save

Depending on what you add to your basic policy, comprehensive homeowner's insurance can add up quickly in price. However, here are some tips to consider if you want to trim your insurance bill:

Raise deductibles. Like other types of insurance, the more you're willing to pay out of pocket before the insurance kicks in, the lower your premiums. Most policies have a $250 deductible—upping that to, say, $2,500 can cut your premiums by one-third. But make sure you have enough cash on hand should you need to meet that deductible.

Bundle policies. It always pays to shop for the best deal you can find. But look into getting homeowner's insurance from the same company that you get auto, life or other insurance from. Many carriers offer multipolicy discounts.

Improve security. Many companies offer premium discounts if you install a home-security system. If that seems too much to pay, improve your home's locks and deadbolts and make sure you have an adequate number of smoke detectors. Those, too, may lower premiums.

Stick with your insurance company. Many carriers begin to cut premiums for customers who've been with them for a while. Finding a solid company and staying with them can ultimately cut your insurance costs.

Consider buying a new home. With many insurers, a new home with brand new wiring and other features is less of a risk than an older home. So, if you're concerned about insurance, a new home may carry lower insurance costs than an older one.

▲ **Don't skimp on homeowner's insurance—it's too important.**

▼ **Don't overlook flood and earthquake protection.**

Other Types
of Insurance

There are forms of insurance other than life, home-owner's and health coverage that are often overlooked by many. But, depending on your circumstances and needs, they may be important to your financial well-being.

Other Options to Consider

Three additional types of insurance—disability, umbrella and renter's—can also provide essential protection.

Disability Insurance

▶ It may be surprising to some, but odds are fairly good that at some point in your working life you'll be physically unable to earn a living due to some sort of accident or illness. That makes disability insurance an essential form of insurance coverage—in essence, it provides you with a form of income in the event you can't do so yourself. While many companies offer disability coverage, many don't, so it's critical to obtain some on your own.

▶ HOW MUCH TO GET: In general, it's a good idea to obtain coverage that will pay between 60 and 80 percent of your current salary.

▶ HOW MUCH THAT MIGHT COST: This will vary according to policies, but a ballpark estimate would be $1,000 in premiums a year for about $12,000 in annual disability payments.

▶ HOW TO REDUCE COSTS: Consider upping the waiting period of your coverage—this is the amount of time after you become disabled and when you get your first disability check. However, if you do that, make sure you have funds from other sources to meet your needs while waiting for the waiting period to expire.

▶ WHAT ELSE TO LOOK FOR: Check to see how long the policy will continue to pay you benefits. If you're concerned about a serious form of disability, look into a policy that pays you up until age 65.

Umbrella Insurance

▶ This type of insurance offers additional liability coverage beyond what homeowner's, renter's, and auto insurance provide. It's a form of protection that can plug certain holes in other types of coverage. For instance, umbrella insurance supplements homeowner's insurance if someone slips on your icy steps and sues you. It can also protect you if someone takes legal action against you stemming from an auto accident.

The Home Office

Be particularly thorough about insurance if you happen to have a home office. Many renter's—and, for that matter, homeowner's policies—provide inadequate coverage for things such as computers, fax machines, and other business tools. Look into specific, additional coverage so that the tools of your home office are sufficiently protected.

Other Types of Insurance Coverage Can Address

Insurance You Don't Need

To this point, we've hit on all sorts of insurance that many people need. Here's a chart of some insurance that, for the lion's share of people, is a thorough waste of money:

Flight Insurance. Granted, this is about as cheap as insurance comes—you can get half a million dollars' coverage for about $20—but it's still inevitably a waste of 20 bucks. Estimates vary, but you probably stand a better chance of winning your state lottery than you have of being involved in a fatal plane crash.

Disease-Specific Insurance. Protecting yourself against things such as cancer and heart disease may seem like a good idea, but this often simply mirrors the coverage that a solid health insurance policy covers already.

Credit Insurance. This is designed to pay a lender—such as a credit card company—in the event you die and leave unpaid debts. Again, that may seem sensible, but it's not. For one thing, that's what life insurance is for. On top of that, you may have sufficient assets to pay off those expenses.

Mortgage Insurance. Again, designed to pay off a mortgage should you die or become disabled. Once more, a good life and/or disability insurance package can adequately address this.

Life Insurance for Children. This is pitched in a lot of places and it's a consummate waste of money—unless, of course, your five-year-old happens to be the primary source of income in your family.

▶ HOW IT WORKS: Umbrella insurance usually has fairly substantial deductibles. The idea is that the insurance takes effect after other forms of coverage are tapped out. So, choose an umbrella policy that leaves little or no gap between coverage provided by other types of insurance.

▶ HOW MUCH IT COSTS: Particularly when compared with other types of insurance, umbrella insurance is dirt cheap. You can usually get $1 million of coverage for a couple hundred dollars a year.

Renter's Insurance

▶ While homeowner's insurance is required to obtain a mortgage, many people who rent overlook the need for renter's insurance—some may assume that their landlord's insurance covers their possessions, which it usually doesn't.

So, if you rent—say you have an apartment in a large city or are temporarily between home purchases—don't bypass renter's insurance.

▶ WHAT IT IS: Renter's insurance offers two forms of protection. First, it protects all your possessions. It also offers a certain amount of liability protection if, for instance, someone is injured on the property.

▶ HOW MUCH TO GET: Make sure you add up the value of everything you own to arrive at a suitable coverage level. Consider replacement value coverage, which takes in how much it might cost to replace something rather than the item's actual value (handy for items that you've owned for a while that, while not particularly valuable, might be costly to replace).

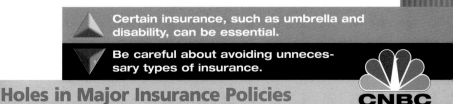

▲ Certain insurance, such as umbrella and disability, can be essential.

▼ Be careful about avoiding unnecessary types of insurance.

Holes in Major Insurance Policies

CNBC

Frequently Asked Questions

Planning and Goals

For long-term goals, is there any way to reduce the risk necessary to achieve financial objectives?

The best way to reduce the risk that you have to take—particularly when targeting long-term goals—is to increase the amount of money you're able to set aside for a particular objective. That way, rather than relying on large total return—something that, unto itself, mandates a certain amount of risk—you can be a bit more conservative. To illustrate:

Scenario 1:
Investing $10,000 a year for 20 years at an 8 percent annual return produces $494,229 at the end of the 20-year period.

Scenario 2:
Investing $5,000 a year for 20 years requires a 14 percent annual return to better the return from the first scenario—in this case, $518,842.

This example shows that, the lower the amount of money invested at the start, the greater the return required to achieve comparable goals—a powerful argument for setting aside as much as possible, particularly when investing for the long haul.

Is diversification more important in a down market?

Some financial pros would argue to the death that that's the case. When, for instance, stocks are heading south, the offsetting benefit from vehicles such as bonds and money markets become essential. In particular, in down markets, some experts say that relatively modest paying investments such as money market accounts—almost an embarrassment when stocks are going up—take on a critical role in generating a reliable return while waiting for conditions to change.

But the better answer is that diversification is critical no matter what the markets happen to be doing. Not everything is going up—or going down—at the same time, so diversification can smooth out the bumps regardless of the direction of the overall market.

How important are taxes when considering long-term goals?

This is akin to the "heat versus humidity" debate. The short answer is that it's always a good idea to consider the impact of taxes. It's particularly critical in determining how much money you'll need to set aside for retirement. That's why vehicles such as IRAs, 401ks, and other sorts of tax-deferred options are so helpful when building a substantial asset base over time.

On the other hand, some pros contend that taxes are over-stated. The argument goes that if the return on your investments is great enough, you come out ahead even if you have to take a significant tax bite. That may be a bit oversimplified, but some-where in the middle of the two positions lies the most compre-hensive answer—keep taxes in mind, but don't obsess over them to the point that you lose sight of your essential investment goals.

How often should you review progress toward long-term financial goals?

The best answer is probably on an annual basis. That way, you can recap how things went, which investments performed as they should, and which ones didn't do quite so well. Even more important, reviewing your long-term portfolio on a yearly basis is a solid way to help determine whether you need to increase the amount of money you're setting aside for a particular goal or if your current funding level is adequate.

Not only is an annual overview handy for seeing what's work-ing as it should, it also helps prevent overreaction. For many investors, too much attention isn't necessarily a good thing. Riv-eted on their investments on a daily basis, they can panic if, say, a mutual fund or stock goes south for a few days. That's by no means enough time to adequately judge an investment's position and prospects. By contrast, looking at a mutual fund annually gives an investor a broader picture—she can see how the fund has performed over time, how it's done versus its peers and, equally important, if something fundamental about the fund has changed that may warrant some sort of action.

Bonds

What factors should an investor consider in choosing between a bond fund and an individual bond?

It really depends on an investor's goals. If, by chance, the investor knows that he can put the money away for some time, knows pretty much when he'll need the money, and targets a high-quality bond, such as a high-rated corporate or municipal bond, then it's suitable to go with the individual bond. On the other hand, bond funds offer greater liquidity. They're ideal for investors who know they'll have to withdraw money incrementally over a period of time. And, like other kinds of funds, bond funds have the advantage of professional management.

Are municipal bonds and bond funds always tax free?

Unfortunately, no. The Internal Revenue Service in recent years has become more aggressive about investigating certain municipal bonds. In some cases, they've determined that the bonds don't comply with tax laws and, as a result, have revoked whatever tax-free status had been in place. That, in turn, has socked investors who thought they were skirting tax with the munis. So be careful—for instance, if you're interested in a municipal-bond fund, ask if any income generated by the fund may be subject to the alternative minimum tax. That may make some of the money paid out to investors taxable.

What is a debenture?

Debentures are a form of corporate bonds. They are very common and are often issued by a company that is restructuring itself financially. That may sound risky, and it is in some cases. In effect, all you're buying with debentures is the credit quality of the company, since a restructuring company may not have any actual assets with which to back a bond. On the other hand, debentures also offer higher rates of return than other bonds, since there's generally a greater amount of risk in play.

Are savings bonds a good idea?

Savings bonds—the tradition-worn gift of choice for kids and graduates—are very similar to zero coupon bonds. They're bought at a deep discount, can never be traded and pay their full (or face) amount at the specified maturity date. On the one hand, they're absolutely safe and their interest is free of state and local taxes. What's more, they're a cheap way to start investing (you can buy them in as little as $25 increments). On the other hand, their returns are really nothing to write home about (as of this writing, the popular EE savings bond is paying 4.5 percent interest).

Does that mean it's important to look at how actively a bond fund is managed?

To a certain extent, yes. Some funds are rather active, as managers move in and out of positions in the hope of latching on to the best returns. Other funds are more like stock index funds—they have relatively little turnover and only try to match the return of a comparable index. It depends largely on what your investment goals are and how aggressive you wish to be. However, the difference between a bond index fund's taxes and taxes paid by a more active fund aren't usually as large as the difference between an active stock fund and a stock index fund. One reason is turnover—a bond fund has to replace a certain number of holdings as bonds mature. A stock index fund, on the other hand, can hold onto a stock indefinitely.

How can I purchase zero coupons and other Treasury Bonds without using a regular stockbroker?

You cannot buy zero coupon bonds without using a stockbroker. Zero coupons were created by brokerage houses and are traded in the secondary market—there is no way to buy these direct without paying some sort of commission or fee to a broker. However, you could try contacting a discount brokerage house, such as Schwab, where you may be able to get away with paying a smaller commission than you would were you to use a larger house.

However, as discussed in the section on bonds, you can buy Treasury bonds directly from the federal government since they are sold at auction on a regular basis.

Mutual Funds

What is a life-cycle mutual fund?

These are funds designed to evolve over time according to an investor's age, investment goals, and other factors. They're usually offered with varying investment philosophies—aggressive, moderate, and conservative—and from there, the funds change their mix. In general, the younger the investor is, the more aggressive the portfolio. As an investor gets older, life-cycle funds are designed to lessen risk and go more toward a conservative approach.

There are several advantages to life-cycle funds. The funds are designed to do the fine-tuning for you—rather than having to tinker with a portfolio to better accommodate needs and goals, the funds are built to do that very thing. That, in turn, automatically imbues investors with good investing habits—instead of being unduly aggressive or conservative, the fund functions to allocate an asset mix that matches the investor's situation. On the downside, life-cycle funds, as a group, can charge higher expense fees. With that in mind, an investor willing to stay on top of a portfolio may do well choosing and managing funds on her own.

Do newly issued mutual funds have the same risks as a stock's initial public offering?

Not really. As a rule, stock IPOs can be exceedingly volatile, often rocketing up in price the minute they start trading and frequently falling back to earth just as quickly. By comparison, new mutual funds don't jump out of the gate in the same way since there aren't investors clamoring for a limited number of shares.

It still pays to be careful with new mutual funds. For one thing, there's no track record to give you any sense of how the fund has performed. Instead, an investor has to look at the manager's prior record with another fund—if that fund is substantially different from the new fund, this can prove a worthless comparison. However, some studies have shown that younger funds occasionally outperform older ones. One theory for that is that the new funds' relatively small size makes management easier and more efficient.

What is a market neutral fund?

It's just what the name implies—rather than betting on the markets to rise or fall, market neutral funds aim right down the middle. Stocks make up half of their portfolios—the other half is allocated to stock shorting and other similar vehicles. The idea is to eliminate the overall effects of market movement but, in the process, profit from short-term ups and downs due to overpriced and underpriced stocks.

Unfortunately, market neutral funds to date have produced spotty results at best. On top of that, since they tend to be highly managed funds, they've also proved to be expensive for investors to own.

Does it ever make sense to own a fund that charges some sort of load?

To judge by other investors, it does. After all, there are millions of investors in funds that levy all sorts of loads. Some investment pros say that it's the fund's performance that truly matters. If a fund with a 4 percent load earns 15 percent a year, it's not hard to figure that it will outperform a no-load fund earning only 8 percent.

So, as a sweeping rule, it's probably the case that you should never dismiss a fund out of hand because it has a load. But know as well that there are scads of no-load funds available that perform just as well as any fund that charges a load. Find one that does, and the issue of whether to pay a load or not becomes a moot point.

Money Market Funds and Certificates of Deposit

Is it better to choose a tax-free money market mutual fund or one that's taxed?

It really depends how much you stand to lose from taxes. Since all income from money market mutual funds comes from dividends, that means they're taxed at the investor's regular income tax level. To counter that, there are some funds that invest in things such as Treasuries and other financial vehicles issued by the government. That, in turn, makes them exempt from state taxes and, in some instances, exempt from federal tax as well.

However, treat these as you would municipal bond funds. Unless you're in a very high tax bracket, it probably doesn't make sense to take the lower returns offered by tax-free money market mutual funds. Instead, go with the higher returns of their conventional counterparts, pay the taxes, and you'll likely come out ahead.

Since they seem similar in so many ways, how do you choose between a certificate of deposit and a money market mutual fund?

The answer boils down to how high a rate of return you want and how soon you may need the money. If you're looking for a better payback, certificates of deposit are generally the way to go. While not a mind-boggling difference, they generally offer higher returns than money market mutual funds, particularly those CDs with longer maturities.

However, if you're unsure when you may need the money or suspect that you may need some of it at some point, opt for the money market mutual funds. CDs levy heavy penalties for early withdrawals. By comparison, money market mutual funds let you make withdrawals, although some funds have rather steep withdrawal minimums.

Is it a bad idea to get into CDs when interest rates are dropping? Aren't you just settling for poor returns?

Not necessarily. For one thing, no matter where you put your short-term funds—in a CD or a money market—they're both going to be hurt by dropping interest rates. In that sense, it's actually a good idea to go with the certificate of deposit, provided you can do without the money for a while. While the money market mutual fund may continue to fall as interest rates decline, a CD at least lets you lock in at a particular rate.

Another thought is to ladder CDs—buy a number with staggered maturity dates. Again, not only are you securing a fixed interest rate but, as the various CDs mature, you're provided with a steady stream of cash to reinvest as you see fit.

What is an "equity linked CD"?

These are a form of certificate of deposit designed to entice investors with greater returns than those offered by conventional CDs. The general idea is that these CDs provide investors with returns akin to what they would get in a stock market index such as the Standard and Poor's 500. Moreover, unlike investing in a basket of stocks, investors are at the very least guaranteed to get back whatever money they put into the CD.

Unfortunately, these CDs have some significant caveats. First off, investors are obligated to tie up their money for a significant amount of time—upwards of 10 years. And, on top of that, returns are tied only to price movement of the index—they don't include dividends, which can be a significant part of a stock's overall return. Add to that the omnipresent concern of a tax bite, and these CDs don't come off quite as rosy as they might appear at first.

IRAs, 401ks, and Stock Options

What is a Keogh Plan and how does it differ from other types of retirement funding plans?

A Keogh Plan is similar to an SEP-IRA in that it is a retirement funding choice for people who are self-employed. One big advantage to Keoghs is that they let you put more money away per year than an SEP does—20 percent of your income, up to an annual maximum of $30,000. Keoghs can also be useful for small employers.

The downside is that, unlike SEPs, Keoghs can be difficult to set up and administer. In fact, most people would need a financial pro to establish a Keogh and to subsequently oversee it on a regular basis. With that in mind, even though a Keogh is more generous with its contributions, the cost of looking after the plan may not make it worthwhile.

What is a Spousal Deductible IRA?

This is yet another variant on the overall IRA theme. If one member of a household has a Keogh or SEP plan and his or her spouse isn't covered by a qualified retirement plan, the spouse can make a deductible IRA contribution up to $2,000. The deduction holds true as long as the family's adjusted gross income doesn't exceed $150,000. After that, the deduction is phased out over the next $10,000 of income.

Is it a good idea to trade stocks and other types of investments in retirement accounts?

In many ways, it is. The biggest ongoing plus is retirement accounts' tax-deferred status. That means, for instance, if you buy and sell stock for profit within an IRA, you won't owe any taxes. The only tax implication comes when you start withdrawing funds at retirement. If, on the other hand, you bought and sold a stock for profit outside a retirement account, you would owe taxes on that profit immediately.

However, bear a couple of considerations in mind. For one thing, if you're actively trading stocks or funds in a retirement account, you're still shelling out commissions, something that eats into the value of your account. And, unlike a nonretirement account, you can't write off any losses from investments that do poorly. So, even with the tax advantages of retirement accounts, there's still a lot to be said for a solid buy-and-hold approach.

What's a variable annuity? Is it a good retirement funding option?

Variable annuities effectively combine a mutual fund with insurance coverage. Investments made into the annuity can grow in value as they would with a mutual fund. Moreover, those funds grow tax-deferred until they're withdrawn. And, on top of that variable annuities—like an insurance policy—also provide a death benefit.

That may seem like an attractive combination, but variable annuities have a number of flaws. For one thing, the death benefit is rather hollow—all it does is guarantee that, should the owner of the annuity die, his or her heirs will either get the account's current value or the initial investment into the account, whichever is greater. Should someone hold an annuity for a long time, it's exceedingly unlikely that the account will have dropped in value.

Another consideration is the expense. As a rule, variable annuities carry much higher operating expenses than comparable mutual funds, costs that cut into investors' returns.

Finally, avoid using a variable annuity within some other type of retirement plan such as a 401k or IRA. You're already enjoying tax-deferred returns from such plans in the first place—that makes the tax-deferred growth of an annuity completely moot.

Brokers, Planners, and Financial Software

In working with a planner or stockbroker, is it a good idea to find other financial professionals on your own, such as estate and tax pros?

In many ways, yes. While one-stop shopping is always convenient—after all, no one really wants to run from office to office, getting some advice here, some advice there—there's something to be said for finding others who have no connection with a planner or broker. The biggest advantage is objectivity—while members of the same firm may take some things for granted (or, in the case of the unscrupulous, overlook things by design), an outsider may notice some things that others might not. For instance, an autonomous tax planner may point out that a certain mutual fund recommended by a planner has an unnecessarily high tax liability. So, finding independent pros on your own may ultimately provide more balance and a better quality of guidance.

Is it ever a good idea to take the chat boards you see at online brokers' sites seriously when researching an investment?

While you should never take chat-board conversation and gossip at face value, they can be useful sources for ideas and leads. For example, an investor may have stumbled across a relatively undervalued stock and is sharing her insights with others on the board. The key is to take that information and do the necessary legwork. Treat chat boards as you would most any other initial source—a font of possibilities that you need to research completely to see if they hold up.

As some investors have discovered to their chagrin, the anonymity of chat boards can effectively hide participants' agendas. As such, you never really know who's doing the talking and why. In some cases, it's perfectly legitimate—interested investors exchanging information with the very best of intentions. In other cases, it's not quite so aboveboard. Some investors may be spreading false information about a stock in hopes of pumping up interest. In fact, several stockbrokers have been caught posing as investors on stock chat boards, feigning enthusiasm about a stock to fuel investor interest.

Are online and software financial-planning tools useful?

They definitely can be. For those unfamiliar with these products and services, there are now a number on Internet-based and software financial-planning programs. Although they differ in their specifics, they generally require that an investor enter information about his financial situation and goals—how much he has saved, his long-term goals, risk tolerance, whether a house purchase or kids' college education are in the mix, and other factors. The systems then return plans that map out what an investor should do.

Depending on the program used, plans can range from rudimentary to exceedingly comprehensive. Some programs go so far as to recommend specific asset allocation breakdowns, particular investments, savings programs, and even insurance coverage. The plans show an investor what he's doing right and what needs to be done to bring things in line with his objectives.

These programs have a couple of built-in pluses. For one thing, they're generally a lot less expensive than working with a broker or planner. And they're designed to function in a purely objective manner. Rather than having a planner pushing commission-based products, financial planning services—at least in theory—are built to give you the straight dope.

The biggest downside is subjectivity. Although programs can offer empirical information, financial planning isn't necessarily an exact science. For instance, even though a program can ask your risk tolerance, it can't see you squirm in your seat when you type in "aggressive." In that sense, a real-life planner or broker can get a feel for an investor's emotional makeup and temperament—something that can play a critical role in how successfully a plan plays out in practice.

After-Hours Trading, International Investing, and Buybacks

How popular is extended-hours trading with individual investors?

To date, extended-hours trading really hasn't taken off with the general investing public. Specific estimates are hard to come by, but there's clear agreement that after-hours trading represents only a nominal fraction of the overall activity on a given trading day. What seems to be holding the system back are the issues of price and liquidity—since there are fewer investors with whom to make trades, it's more difficult to execute a trade at a genuinely attractive price.

Nor, it's interesting to note, is the United States the only marketplace to experience sluggish after-hours trading activity. The Milan stock exchange, for instance, recently canceled plans to extend after-hours trading, citing little investor interest. Other stock markets have taken a different strategy to stimulate investor activity—the Frankfurt market chose to extend the hours of its normal trading day into the evening rather than institute an after-hours program.

What's the difference between an international fund and a global fund?

As discussed in the section on international investing, names can often be very misleading so far as knowing precisely where a fund is putting its money. This is a case in point. International funds, by design, only invest in foreign stocks. By comparison, global funds may also earmark a portion of their portfolios for domestic companies.

That may seem like an exercise in pure semantics, but it can have a very real effect on your investing strategy. For instance, if an investor is 70 percent invested in American stocks and, fearing a recession, wants to put the remainder of her portfolio overseas, an international fund would be the suitable choice. However, if the investor went with a global fund thinking that her portfolio was adequately diversified, she would have increased her domestic holdings. So, it's important to make certain that a fund's strategy matches your investment ideas.

Do domestic mutual funds set aside a portion of their portfolios for overseas investments?

Absolutely. Domestic funds routinely earmark a portion of their holdings for international stocks and bonds. So it's a good idea before investing in internationally focused funds to check the holdings of the funds you already own. You may be surprised to find that you're already deeper into international waters than you may have thought.

What's a stock buyback? Isn't that a sort of insider activity on a particularly large scale?

Not really. Stock buybacks are essentially rather simple. A company buys back its own shares on the open market, much like an investor loading up on a particularly large number of shares. A stock buyback can often be interpreted as a good sign for other investors who already own shares in a company. Like an insider buying significant blocs of shares, a company stock buyback can be an indicator of optimism in the company's future prospects. After all, like any other sort of investor, the company wouldn't be laying out its cash if it wasn't reasonably sure that the money was going into a solid investment.

However, company stock buybacks aren't always a slam dunk for investors. Perhaps the biggest concern is an unwise use of funds—in some cases, a company that bought back its own stock could, in fact, have better used that money elsewhere. Analysts urge that company buybacks be taken as part of a company's total picture, not just one development that overrides other considerations such as price-earnings ratios, sales, and other elementary considerations.

Futures and Options

In trading futures, what's the difference between hedging and speculating?

The essential difference boils down to whether an investor is looking to protect a position or to profit from a position. Hedging refers to the buying and selling of futures contracts to offset the risks of changing prices. Big producers or users of a commodity use futures to hedge their price exposure. Speculating, on the other hand, means the investor is willing to take on the risk of futures to try to make a profit. So hedging is more defensive in nature, while speculating is more aggressive. However, they do serve to balance the overall market.

Investors pay a premium to buy an option. How is the price calculated?

It's very much like the trading floor on a stock exchange. Premiums are determined by brokers representing both buyers and sellers who dicker until they arrive at a fair price. And, like stock exchanges, options markets are federally regulated—in this case, by the Commodity Futures Trading Commission (CFTC). There are also several industry groups.

What is a LEAP?

A LEAP (a registered trademark of the Chicago Board Options Exchange) stands for a Long-Term Equity Anticipation Security. In essence, it's an option, but it has a much longer term than traditional stock or index options—about two and one-half years and sometimes even longer. Like options, a stock-related LEAP may be a call or a put, meaning that the owner has the right to purchase or sell shares of the stock at a given price on or before some prespecified date.

What's the difference between so-called European-style options and an American-style option?

The difference boils down to the time at which an option may be exercised. With a European-style option, an investor can exercise the option only during a specified period of time. This occurs just before the option is slated to expire. An American-style option, by contrast, can be exercised at any time prior to its expiration date.

What does the term "fence" mean?

This is a fairly involved strategy that can be useful in protecting stock profits. The strategy involves an investor taking a written call as well as a long put against a stock that she already owns. This establishes what's known as a "collar"—no matter which way the stock may move, the investor is protected by both the call and the put. In this manner the profits the stock has already realized are also protected.

Investment and Money Management

Here are some more frequently asked questions having to do with investing and money management.

How can we track down information about an old stock certificate or one connected with a company that seems to have completely dropped out of sight?

There are a number of companies that investigate these sorts of stocks for a fee. One of them is R.M. Smythe (800-622-1880). Smythe offers this kind of service for a fee of $75 per company. To research a company, any sort of information is helpful, such as where a company might be located or when the stock was bought.

Another possibility would be to take the stock certificates to a full-service brokerage house to see if they can track down any information about the company—ask for the old-issues department or some similarly named department. If you have an account or work with a broker there, they'll probably do this for free, although you would likely have to pay a commission if you decide to liquidate the stocks.

Can I roll my SEP into a 401k?

The answer is yes. Once you're employed by a company, SEPs can be rolled over into 401ks. However, it's probably a good idea to check with the 401k plan administrator at your new job to make sure that particular 401k plan does, in fact, permit that sort of rollover. Various plans have all sorts of rules as to what employees can and cannot do.

However, perhaps the more important question is why you would want to do this. SEPs allow you to choose virtually any sort of investment vehicle that you wish for your money. By comparison, many 401ks offer only a few investment options, and some programs are notorious for offering poor performing choices. Additionally, once the money is in the 401k, it has to remain there until you move on to another job. Additionally, if you're weary of paying the yearly fee to administer the SEP, simply transfer the account to a discount brokerage house. That should greatly trim that expense and allow you to keep your SEP funds unaffected by the limitations of a 401k.

Can you undo a UGMA account?

Yes. Should you wish to dismantle a UGMA account, you can simply start spending the money that's in the account. The money must be spent "for the child's benefit"—according to the IRS, this can mean anything from food, lodging, clothing, transportation, recreation and other necessities. However, the money may not be used for things such as taxes and life insurance premiums.

There are drawbacks to this. For one thing, a parent or guardian spending down the account will be liable for taxes on any interest, dividends, or capital gains the money may have earned while in the UGMA—these will be taxed at the parent's rate. Additionally, you may have to explain to the Internal Revenue Service why the account is being closed and just how the proceeds are being spent. Lastly, it's not inconceivable that the child may choose to sue the parent or guardian who is closing down the account because he or she is ostensibly taking money back that legally belongs to the child.

There is another alternative, albeit a rather involved and costly one. If the amount of money in the account is substantial, you may want to investigate setting up a Family Limited Partnership and transferring the UGMA funds into that. Under a Family Limited Partnership, the child can retain ownership of the money, with someone else (most likely the parents) serving as managing partner or partners. As such, the money remains the child's but the parents as managing partners control all monies in the trust. This may be the solution if you're concerned about what a child will do with the money in the UGMA once he comes of age. However, a Family Limited Partnership costs a couple thousand dollars to set up, so whatever is in the UGMA should be substantial enough to justify that kind of expense. Also, check to make sure that such a transfer is legal in the state where you live.

Retirement Accounts and Banking

More questions and answers dealing with investing, saving, retirement planning, and other financial issues.

My employer takes money from my paycheck for my 401k every two weeks, but only deposits the money in my 401k every month. In the meantime, my money just sits there. Is this legal, and is there anything I can do about it?

It is very common for employers to deposit 401k contributions less frequently than they receive them from employees. The law stipulates that employers have until the fifteenth business day of the month following the withholding to deposit the funds into the 401k account. For most employers, it's probably just a matter of convenience—it's easier to make fewer, larger deposits than a greater number of smaller ones.

The only thing you can do is ask your employer if he'd consider a more frequent deposit schedule. Other than that, you have no real recourse. However, it's better that the money sit there rather than being placed in an interest-bearing account on your behalf because any interest earned on the money would then have to classified as profit sharing, which would only make things more complicated. Moreover, you're not really losing all that much: for a monthly 401k deposit totaling $350, that money placed in an account earning 5 percent would produce under $2 a month. So you're not taking all that big a hit by having the money remain in limbo for a short time.

How can I shop for banking services that won't end up costing me an arm and a leg?

Here's a list of shopping strategies:

• First, ask your bank for a complete schedule of charges and fees. Be scrupulous about this—for instance, banks have increased their fees for overdrafts and monthly maintenance fees. Some banks charge you every time you use a teller for a transaction instead of an ATM. Others levy surcharges if you use a blank counter slip to withdraw money instead of preprinted withdrawal slips. So, check out the fee structure to see what various services will cost you. In particular, watch for "bundling," wherein your bank sells you a service you may not necessarily want in exchange for a slightly lower fee on another service.

• Keep things as simple as you can. Find the lowest-cost checking account possible—if you write lots of checks, look for one that charges a flat monthly fee. If you write relatively few, an account based on a per check fee may be cheaper.

• It's a good idea to keep as little money in your checking account as possible, since if it's earning no interest in a simple checking account, it does you no good. As a rule, try not to have more than two to three months' living expenses in your account. And, bypass interest-bearing checking and conventional savings accounts, whose returns are dreadful. Instead, put your excess cash in a money market mutual fund, whose returns are better than everyday savings and interest-bearing checking. Once that's in place, keep your money in there as long as possible, and move it into checking and investments as you need it.

• Pay attention to other fees and services. Track how often you use your ATM card in a given month. If your bank charges per ATM transaction (or levies steep fees for ATM transactions at other locations), look into another bank. If you're interested in an account where a minimum balance eliminates monthly fees, make sure you understand just what the bank means by a mini-mum—some banks average out the balance over the entire month, while others will levy fees even if the balance drops below the minimum for just a day or so.

Glossary

A

Accountant's opinion:
Signed statement of opinion from an accounting firm on a corporation's financial statements. The auditor must follow generally accepted accounting principles. The opinion can be unqualified or qualified. A qualified opinion calls attention to limitations of the audit or unusual items in the statement.

Accounts payable: Money a company owes for merchandise or services bought on credit.

Accounts receivable:
Money owed to a company for merchandise or services bought on credit.

Accrual basis: Accounting method in which income and expenses are accounted for as they are earned or incurred, although they may not have been received or paid yet.

Adjusted gross income (AGI): A measure used to calculate how much income is taxable by the government. AGI is calculated with gross income from taxable sources minus certain items, such as payments to a Keogh plan or a deductible Individual Retirement Account (IRA). AGI minus deductions and personal exemptions is taxable income.

Affiliate: An association between two companies when one owns less than a majority stake of the other, or when both are subsidiaries of a third company. Or, generally, any association between two companies that is short of a parent-subsidiary tie.

After-hours trading: Real-time trading that takes place outside the normal exchange hours of 9:30 a.m. to 4 p.m. Eastern Standard Time. With after-hours systems, buyers and sellers may transact business before the markets open as well as after the markets have closed.

Aggregate: A total amount.

Alternative minimum tax (AMT): Tax-law provision that ensures that individuals and companies pay some income tax, no matter how many deductions or credits they claim. Under the AMT, money not usually considered taxable (such as income on tax-free bonds) and sums considered usually deductible are treated as taxable.

American depositary receipts (ADRs): Receipts held by an American bank that represent shares in a foreign company. Also called American depositary shares.

American Stock Exchange (AMEX): Third most active market in the U.S., behind the New York Stock Exchange and the Nasdaq Stock Market. The exchange was founded in 1842 in New York City. Most stocks traded on it are those of small- to mid-sized companies.

American-style option: An option that may be exercised on or before the expiration date.

Amex Composite Index: Index that measures the aggregate value of all Amex-listed stocks.

Amortization: Accounting procedure that companies use to write off intangible rights or assets—such as goodwill, patents, or copyrights—over the period of their existence.

Annual effective yield: Measure of the actual annual return on an account after interest is compounded.

Annual percentage rate (APR): Interest rate that borrowers pay on a loan. Most of a loan's up-front fees are factored into the APR.

Annual report: Yearly report on a company's financial state and organization that is prepared by management for shareholders.

Annuity: An investment contract whereby an individual makes an upfront payment now in return for a stream of monthly income in the future. It is offered by insurers, banks, brokerage firms and mutual fund companies and is commonly used to save on a tax-deferred basis for retirement.

Antitrust law: Any law that encourages competition by limiting unfair business practices and curbing monopolies' power.

Appreciate: An increase in an asset's value.

Arbitrage: Buying and selling securities simultaneously to take advantage of price differences. E.g., buying gold in London and selling it in New York; buying a basket of stocks that make up an index and selling the index itself.

Asked: Price being sought for a security by the seller. Also called the offer.

Asset: Everything a company or individual owns or is owed.

Asset allocation: Investment technique of dividing investment money among a variety of instruments and markets.

Asset-backed securities: Securities backed by loans or accounts receivable. For example, an asset-backed bond is created when a securities firm bundles some type of debt, like car loans, and sells investors the right to receive the payments that consumers make on those loans.

Asset-management accounts: All-in-one accounts that allow customers of brokerage firms to buy and sell securities and store cash in one or more money market mutual funds. Asset-management accounts generally offer check-writing privileges, credit or debit cards, and automatic transfers from one account to another. They often come with an annual fee of up to $100.

At-the-money: An option with a strike price equal to the current price of the instrument, such as a stock, upon which the option was granted.

Auction market: Trading securities on a stock exchange where buyers compete with other buyers and sellers compete with other sellers for the best stock price. Trading in individual stocks is managed and kept orderly by a specialist.

Auditor's report: Independent accounting firm's opinion on whether the company's financial statements conform to generally accepted accounting principles.

Average annual yield: Measure of the return on investments of more than one year. It is calculated by adding each year's return on investment and dividing that number by the number of years invested.

Averages: In the stock market, averages are indicators that measure price changes in representative stock prices. The most popular indicator is the Dow Jones Industrial Average, which measures the performance of 30 industrial stocks.

B

Balance sheet: Financial statement that lists a company's assets and liabilities as of a specified date.

Balanced fund: Mutual fund that has three investment objectives: conserve the investors' principal, pay steady income and promote long-term growth of both principal and income.

Bankruptcy: Legal process governed by the U.S. bankruptcy code for people or companies unable to meet financial obligations. The bankruptcy code is divided into chapters that provide different types of relief. Chapter 7 governs liquidation rather than reorganization. Chapter 11 provides for reorganization and repayment for individuals, partnerships, and corporations that are domiciled in the U.S. Chapter 13 provides for individual debt adjustments and is an alternative to liquidation under Chapter 7.

Basis point: Smallest measure used in quoting yields on bonds and notes. One basis point is 0.01 percent of yield. For example, a bond's yield that changed from 12.72 percent to 12.52 percent has moved 20 basis points.

Bearer stock: Stock certificates that aren't registered in any name. They are negotiable without endorsement by any person.

Bear market: When security prices decline 15 percent or more.

Beneficiary: A person named to receive a benefit in a will, life insurance policy, retirement plan, or other financial arrangement upon death.

Beta: An estimate of an investment's volatility. The lower the beta, the less risky the investment.

Bid: The highest price that someone is willing to pay for a security or an asset.

Big Board: Another name for the New York Stock Exchange.

Bill of exchange: Signed, written order by one business that instructs another business to pay a third business a specific amount. Also called a draft.

Block trade: Buying or selling 10,000 shares of stock or $200,000 or more worth of bonds.

Blue-chip stocks: Stocks of companies known for their long-established record of earning profits and paying dividends.

Bond: Debt instrument that pays a set amount of interest on a regular basis. The issuer promises to repay the debt on time and in full. Bonds are bought and sold on the secondary market.

Bond Buyer Municipal Bond Index: An index based on 40 long-term municipal bonds that is often used to track the performance of tax-free municipal bonds. The index is compiled by *The Bond Buyer*, a trade publication.

Bond rating (debt rating): An assessment of the likelihood that investors will receive the promised interest and principal payments on time. Bond ratings are assigned by independent agencies, such as Moody's Investors Service and Standard & Poor's.

Book-to-bill ratio: A measure of sales trends of a company or industry. A number above 1 indicates an expanding market, and a number below 1 is a contracting market. For example, a book-to-bill ratio of 1.03 means that for every $100 of products shipped, $103 in new orders was received.

Book value: A company's net worth (difference between a company's assets and its liabilities), usually expressed in per-share terms.

Bottom fishing: Buying stocks whose prices have bottomed out or fallen to low levels.

Bottom line: Accounting term for the net profit or loss.

Brady bonds: Securities issued by foreign governments as part of a debt-restructuring program initiated by former U.S. Treasury Secretary Nicholas Brady.

Broker: A person who gives advice and handles orders to buy or sell stocks, bonds, commodities, and options.

Brokerage firm: Financial-services firm that provides the service of buying and selling securities. Brokerage firms fall into two main camps, full-service brokers and discount brokers.

Bull market: A time period when securities prices increase.

C

Cafeteria plan: Flexible-benefit plan offered by many employers that gives workers a certain number of credits and a menu of benefit options on which to spend them. The list may include medical coverage, life insurance, disability coverage, vacation days, and dental care. Employees who do not want a particular benefit can spend more on another, or receive the difference in cash.

Call: Issuer's right to redeem a bond or preferred share before it matures.

Callable bond: A bond that can be redeemed by the issuer before it matures.

Call option: Agreement that gives an investor the right but not the obligation to buy a stock, bond, commodity, or other instrument at a specified price within a specific time period.

Call risk: The risk that an issuer may redeem a security sooner than expected.

Capital asset: An asset held for more than a year that isn't bought or sold in the normal course of business. Capital assets generally include fixed assets, such as land, buildings, equipment, and furniture.

Capital gain: Difference between the purchase price and the sale price of an asset when the asset was sold for more than it was bought.

Capital loss: Difference between the purchase price and the sale price of an asset when the asset was sold for less than it was bought.

Cash flow: Net income after depreciation and other noncash charges are included.

Cash market: The trading of securities according to their current—or spot—price. That is in contrast to trading in a security for future delivery.

Certificate of deposit: A savings contract that pays a fixed interest rate for a specified time.

Certified Financial Planner (CFP): The best-known financial planning designation, given to qualifying planners by the CFP Board of Standards of Denver.

Certified Public Accountant (CPA): An accountant who has passed an administered examination that focuses on accounting practices and taxes.

Charitable lead trust: A trust that pays a charity income from a donated asset for a set number of years, after which time the principal goes to the donor's beneficiaries with reduced estate or gift taxes.

Charitable remainder trust: A trust that allows people to leave assets to a charity and receive a tax break but still retain income for life. This works best for people with a large appreciated asset, which, if sold, would generate large capital-gains taxes.

Chartered Financial Analyst (CFA): This qualification focuses on portfolio management and securities analysis. It also covers economics, financial accounting, securities analysis and standards of conduct.

Chartered Financial Consultant (ChFC): Financial planning designation given to qualifying planners by the American College of Bryn Mawr, Pennsylvania.

Chartered Life Underwriter (CLU): A professional designation given to qualifying life insurance agents by the American College of Bryn Mawr, Pennsylvania.

Chicago Board of Trade (CBOT): One of the oldest futures exchanges where agricultural and financial futures and options are traded.

Chicago Board Options Exchange (CBOE): An exchange set up by the Chicago Board of Trade to trade stock options. It now has trading in a variety of options contracts including options on stock indices, interest rates and sector indices.

Churning: Excessive trading in a customer's brokerage account, done to generate increased commission income. Churning is a securities law violation. In the stock market, it refers to a period of heavy trading activity but few sustained price trends and little overall movement in stock market indexes.

Circuit breakers: Measures used by some major stock and commodities exchanges to restrict trading temporarily when markets rise or fall too far and/or too fast.

Closed-end fund: Type of fund that issues a set number of shares and typically trades on a stock exchange.

Closely held: Companies in which stock and voting control are concentrated in the hands of a few investors, although the companies' shares may be traded to a limited extent.

Closing price: The last traded price of a stock when the market closes.

Collaborative fund: Also known as collective intelligence funds. While these are managed by professionals, they choose the makeup of the portfolio based on recommendations from volunteer stock pickers.

Collateral: Stock or other property that borrowers are obliged to turn over to lenders if they are unable to repay a loan.

Collateralized Mortgage Obligations (CMOs): Multi-class bond backed by a pool of mortgage pass-through securities or mortgage loans.

Commercial bank: A bank owned by shareholders that accepts deposits, makes commercial and industrial loans, and provides other banking services to the public. Also called a full-service bank.

Commercial paper: Unsecured short-term promissory notes used by companies to obtain cash. They are sold through dealers in the open market or directly to investors.

Commodities: Bulk goods such as grains, metals, livestock, oil, cotton, coffee, sugar, and cocoa. They can either be sold on the spot market for immediate delivery or on the commodities exchanges for later delivery. Trade on the exchanges is in the form of futures contracts.

Common stock: Represents part ownership of a company. Holders of common stock have voting rights but no guarantee of dividend payments.

Composite trading: Total amount of trading across all markets in a share that is listed on the New York Stock Exchange or American Stock Exchange. This includes transactions on those exchanges, the five regional exchanges and on the Nasdaq Stock Market.

Compounding: If your investments make 10 percent a year for five years, you earn not 50 percent but 61.1 percent. Here is the reason: as time goes on, you make money not only on your original investment but also on your accumulated gains from earlier years.

Comptroller of the Currency: A Treasury Department official, appointed by the president and confirmed by the Senate, who is responsible for chartering, examining, supervising, and liquidating national banks.

Consumer credit: Money loaned to individuals, usually on an unsecured basis, requiring monthly repayment. Bank loans, credit cards, and installment credit are examples of consumer credit.

Consumer price index (CPI): A gauge of inflation that measures changes in the prices of consumer goods. The index is based on a list of specific goods and services purchased in urban areas. It is released monthly by the Labor Department.

Convertible bond: A bond that investors may exchange for stock at some future date under certain conditions.

Corporate bonds: Bonds issued by corporations.

Corporation: A business entity treated as a person in the eyes of the law. It is able to own property, incur debts, sue, and be sued.

Correction: A reverse movement, usually downward, in the price of an individual stock, bond, commodity, index, or the stock market as a whole.

Cost basis: In accounting, the valuation of an asset that includes the cost of the asset and factors in items like depreciation, capital gains, and dividends.

Cost of living: Level of prices of goods and services required for a reasonable standard of living.

Cost-push inflation: A sustained rise in prices caused by businesses passing on increases in costs, especially labor costs, to purchasers.

Coupon: The interest rate specified on a bond when it is originally issued.

Covered: An investment strategy in which the seller owns the underlying security.

Credit ratings: Formal evaluation of a government or company's credit history and ability to repay its debts.

"Curbs In": An indication that trading curbs have been installed on the New York Stock Exchange.

Currency: Money that circulates in an economy. Also refers to a country's official unit of exchange.

Current ratio: A measure of a company's liquidity, or its ability to pay its short-term debts. Calculated by dividing current assets by current liabilities.

Current yield: A measure of an investor's return on a bond. Calculated by dividing the coupon rate by the purchase price, then multiplying by $1,000.

Cyclical stocks: Shares that tend to rise during an upturn in the economy and fall during a downturn.

D

Day order: An investor's order to buy or sell that will be canceled by the end of the day if not filled.

Debenture: A bond backed only by a corporation's good credit, not by specific collateral.

Debt: Securities such as bonds, notes, mortgages, and other forms of paper that indicate the intent to repay an amount owed.

Default: Failure to pay principal or interest on a financial obligation. It can also refer to a breach or nonperformance of the terms of a debt instrument.

Defensive securities: Stock of companies whose earnings tend to grow despite the business cycle (e.g., food and drug firms), or of companies that pay relatively high dividends, like utilities.

Deflation: A decline in the general price level of goods and services that results in increased purchasing power of money. The opposite of inflation.

Delta: A measure of the price-change relationship between an option and its underlying asset.

Depreciation: A decline in value. In accounting, a reduction of earnings to write off the cost of an asset over its estimated useful life.

Depression: A severe downturn in an economy that is marked by falling prices, reduced purchasing power, and high unemployment.

Derivative: A financial product whose value is derived from an underlying financial asset, such as stocks, bonds, currencies or mortgages. Derivatives may be listed on exchanges or traded privately over-the-counter. For example, derivatives may be futures, options, or mortgage-backed securities.

Direct Purchase Plans (DPP): Direct Purchase Plans allow you to buy stock directly from the company that issues the stock.

Discount: In general, the amount by which one security price is less than another. In financing, it is the interest withheld when a note, draft, or bill is purchased.

Discount brokers: Brokers who charge lower commissions than full-service brokers and usually limit their service to trade execution.

Discount rate: The interest rate charged by the Federal Reserve on loans to banks.

Disinflation: A slowdown in the rate of price increases. Disinflation occurs during a recession, when sales drop and retailers are unable to pass higher prices along to consumers.

Diversification: Spreading investments among different types of securities to lessen risk.

Dividend Reinvestment Plans (DRIPs): A program offered by companies to allow the automatic reinvestment of stockholder dividends in additional shares.

Dividends: A portion of a company's income paid to shareholders as a return on their investment.

Dividend yield: A company's annual dividend expressed as a percentage of its current stock price.

Dollar-cost averaging: A strategy to invest fixed amounts of money in securities at regular intervals, regardless of the market's movements.

Dow Jones averages: There are four Dow Jones averages that track price changes in various sectors. The Dow Jones Industrial Average tracks the price changes of the stock of 30 industrial companies. The Dow Jones Transportation Average monitors the price changes of the stocks of 20 airlines, railroads and trucking companies. The Dow Jones Utility Average measures the performance of the stock of 15 gas, electric and power companies. The Dow Jones 65 Composite Average monitors the stock of all 65 companies that make up the other three averages.

Dow Jones Equity Market Index: Index that measures price changes in more than 100 U.S. industry groups. The stocks in the index represent about 80 percent of U.S. market capitalization and trade on the New York Stock Exchange, the American Stock Exchange, and the Nasdaq Stock Market. The equity-market index is market-capitalization weighted, which means that a stock's influence on the index is proportionate to its size in the market.

Dow Jones Global Indexes: Some 2,700 companies' stocks in 29 countries worldwide are tracked by geographic region and by 120 industry groups. Collectively, they represent more than 80 percent of the equity capital on stock markets around the world. All of the indexes are weighted by market capitalization, which is the product of price times shares outstanding. Thus, each country carries a weight proportionate to the relative value of its equities the total value of world equities. The U.S. market is the world's biggest, and the U.S. component of the global indexes has the most stocks—more than 700.

Dow Jones Industrial Average (DJIA): Often referred to as the Dow, this is the best known and most widely reported indicator of the stock market's performance. The Dow tracks the price changes of 30 mostly industrial stocks traded on the New York Stock Exchange. Their combined market value is roughly equal to 20 percent of the market value of all U.S. stocks and 25 percent of those listed on the New York Stock Exchange.

Dow Jones World Stock Index: An index that measures the performance of more than 2,000 companies worldwide that represent more than 80 percent of the equity capital on 25 stock markets.

Duration: A calculation measuring the expected life of a fixed-income security. It estimates the time required to collect a fixed-income security's payments of the principal and interest.

E

Earnings: Income after a company's taxes and all other expenses have been paid. Also called profit or net income.

Earnings per share: The amount of earnings allocated to each share of common stock. Calculated by dividing earnings by the number of shares outstanding.

Earnings yield: A company's per-share earnings expressed as a percentage of its stock price. This provides a yardstick for comparing stocks with bonds, as well as with other stocks.

Economic indicators: Key statistics used to analyze business conditions and make forecasts.

Education IRA: Education IRAs are available to help finance a child's education. Contributions of up to $2,000 may be made in any given year, depending on income. Now called the Coverdell Education Savings Account.

Emerging markets: Financial markets in nations that are developing market-based economies, such as in Latin American and China.

Employee Stock Ownership Plan (ESOP): A program encouraging employees to buy stock in their company and thereby have a greater stake in its financial performance.

Equity: In property, it is the difference between the property's current market value and the claims against the property. In securities markets, it is the part of a company's net worth that belongs to shareholders.

Estate taxes: Taxes levied by the federal and state governments on the transfer of your assets after you die. Uncle Sam levies estate taxes on the worldwide assets of both U.S. citizens and U.S. residents.

Euro: The currency of the 12 countries in the new European Union.

Eurobonds: Corporate or government bond denominated in a currency other than the currency of the issuer.

Eurocurrency: Any currency held in a bank outside the country of origin.

Eurodollars: Dollar-denominated deposits in banks outside the U.S.

European-style option: An option that may be exercised only on its expiration date.

European Union: An intergovernmental organization of 15 Western European nations created under the Maastricht treaty of December 1991 with its own institutional structures and decision-making framework. Before the Maastricht treaty went into effect in November 1993, the organization was known as the European Community or the Common Market. Its members are Austria, Belgium, Denmark, Finland, France, Germany, Greece, Ireland, Italy, Luxembourg, the Netherlands, Portugal, Spain, Sweden, and the United Kingdom. Its council of ministers and the European Commission are based in Brussels, Belgium, and its parliament is based in Strasbourg, France. Also called the EU.

Exchange: A centralized place for trading securities and commodities, usually involving an auction process.

Exchange Traded Funds (ETFs): Similar to regular mutual funds, these track major indices. Unlike mutual funds which can only transact business at the end of the day, exchange traded funds can be bought or sold at any time. Also, unlike a mutual fund, an ETF can be sold short and bought on margin.

Ex-dividend: The time period between the announcement and the payment of a dividend. New investors in the stock in this period are not entitled to receive the dividend the stock trades lower than on the first day of this time. On that day the stock is said to go ex-dividend.

Executor: The person named in a will to handle the settlement of the estate.

Expense ratio: This figure tells you how much a mutual fund charges each year as a percentage of total fund assets. A fund with a 1.55 percent expense ratio, for instance, levies $1.55 for every $100 it has under management. Included in this figure are the fund's management fee, shareholder servicing costs, and any annual 12b-1 fee. A 12b-1 fee, which is named after the applicable Securities and Exchange Commission regulation, is levied to pay for the cost of attracting new investors to the fund. The fee may be used to buy advertising or to compensate brokers who sell the fund.

Expiration date: The date after which an option may no longer be exercised.

F

Face value: The monetary value of a bond printed on its face. Face value and market value often differ.

Fair value: A mathematical relationship between the futures and the S&P 500 index.

Federal debt: The amount of debt sold by the federal government to fund past deficits.

Federal deficit: Money owed by the federal government when spending exceeds tax revenues collected.

Federal funds rate: The interest rate banks charge on overnight loans to banks that need more cash to meet bank reserve requirements. The Federal Reserve sets the interest rate.

Federal Reserve: The central bank of the U.S. that sets monetary policy. The Federal Reserve oversees money supply, interest rates, and credit with the goal of keeping the U.S. economy and currency stable. Governed by a seven-member board, the system includes 12 regional Federal Reserve Banks, 25 branches, and all national and state banks that are part of the system. Also called the Fed.

Financial planner: A type of financial adviser, ideally one with broad knowledge of all areas of personal finance. But no particular training or credentials are required of investment and insurance products.

Fiscal year: The 12-month period that a corporation or government uses for bookkeeping purposes.

529 College Savings Plan: Managed by individual states, 529 plans let adults earmark large upfront contributions for college—up to $250,000, depending on the individual state plan.

Flexible spending account: An employee benefit offered by many companies that allows employees to have pretax dollars withheld from their salaries to pay for unreimbursed medical expenses and dependent-care expenses, such as babysitting or elder care.

Float: In securities, the number of outstanding shares in a corporation available for trading by the public. Also, the time between the deposit of a check in a bank and the check's payment.

Floater: An insurance policy that covers specific items of personal property, such as jewelry.

Floating an issue: Offering stocks or bonds to the public for the first time. It can be an initial public offering or an offering of issues by companies that are already public.

Foreign exchange: Money instruments used to make payments between countries.

Foreign exchange market: Market in which foreign currencies are bought and sold and exchange rates between currencies are determined.

Forward exchange rate: A currency exchange contract that traders have agreed upon for a future date. The forward rate is usually for one, two, three, or six months, and is referred to as 30-day forward, 60-day forward, etc.

Forward trading: Trade, usually at the current price, in which actual delivery and settlement is made at a future date. Forward trade occurs in the commodity, foreign exchange, stock, bond, and futures markets.

401k plan: An employer-sponsored retirement-savings plan funded by employees with contributions that are deducted from pretax pay. Employers frequently add matching contributions up to a set limit.

403(b) plan: A retirement-savings plan for employees of colleges, hospitals, school districts, and nonprofit organizations. The plan, which is similar to the 401k plan offered to many corporate employees, is funded by employees with contributions that are deducted from pretax pay.

Friendly takeover: An acquisition of one company by another in which the boards of both companies agree to the terms of the transaction.

Full-service brokers: Brokers who execute buy and sell orders, research investments, help investors develop and meet investment goals, and give advice to investors. They charge commissions for their work.

Fundamental analysis: Analysis technique that looks at a company's financial condition, management, and place in its industry to predict its stock price movement.

Funds of funds: Funds of funds take proceeds from investors and, in turn, invest that money into other mutual funds.

Futures: An agreement to purchase or sell a given quantity of a commodity, security, or currency at a specified date in the future. Also called a futures contract.

Futures option: An option on a futures contract.

G

General-obligation bond:
A municipal government bond that is approved either by the voters or their legislature. The government's promise to repay the principal and pay the interest is constitutionally guaranteed, based on its ability to tax the population.

Gift tax: Federal taxes owed on gifts if they exceed both the annual limit of $10,000 per recipient and the $600,000 lifetime unified credit.

Gross domestic product (GDP): The total value of goods and services produced by a nation. In the U.S. it is calculated by the Commerce Department, and it is the main measure of U.S. economic output.

Gross spread: The difference between the price that investors are charged for the security, and the amount of proceeds that are paid to the issuer.

Growth: This word label is applied both to a type of mutual fund and to a style of investing. Growth funds invest for capital gains—the profit that you make when you sell an investment for more than your cost. But these funds do not necessarily use the growth-stock investment style, which involves buying stocks that may have little or nothing in the way of current earnings but have the potential for rapid earnings growth.

Growth fund: A mutual fund that invests in the common stock of well-established companies. The aim of a growth fund is to buy stocks whose share price will increase over time.

Guaranteed investment contracts (GICs): Investments offered by insurance companies that promise preservation of principal and a fixed rate of return. Individuals invest in GICs through 401ks and other retirement plans.

H

Hard assets: Also known as tangible assets, these investments tend to perform well when the inflation rate is picking up. Gold and other precious metals are among the best-known hard assets.

Hedge funds: Little-regulated private investment partnerships for large investors. They wager huge sums in global currency, bond and stock markets.

Hedging: Buying or selling a product or a security to offset a possible loss from adverse movements in securities prices or interest rates.

Home-equity debt: Borrowing secured by a homeowner's equity in a home. Home-equity loans allow you to borrow a certain amount and pay it back over a specified term, and they generally carry fixed interest rates. Home-equity lines of credit allow you to draw upon them as needed, and they usually carry adjustable rates.

Hostile takeover: An acquisition of one company by another over the objections of the target company's board. Often an acquirer will take its transaction directly to the shareholders of the target company, offering to buy their shares through a tender offer, or seeking their approval to remove opposing members from the target company's board.

Hot issue: A stock that attracts attention because its share price has risen substantially, and in many cases is expected to rise further.

I

Incentive stock options:
A compensation plan that gives executives the right to purchase stock at a specified price during a specific period of time. The options are free of tax when they

are granted and when they are exercised.

Income bond fund: A mutual fund that seeks a high level of steady income by investing in a mix of corporate and government bonds.

Income equity fund: A mutual fund that seeks a high level of steady income by investing in stocks of companies with consistent records of paying dividends.

Income fund: A mutual fund that seeks a high level of current income by investing in income-producing securities, including both stocks and bonds. Certain types of stocks that generate income are also known as income stocks.

Income statement and balance sheet: Located inside a company's annual report, the income statement and balance sheet are a comprehensive itemization of the company's financial activities.

Index arbitrage: Buying or selling baskets of stocks while at the same time executing offsetting trades in stock-index futures. For exa... ...stocks are temporaril... ...er than futures an arbitr... ...buy stocks and sell future... ...ture a profit on the differ... ...spread between the two...

Ind... ...nd: A mutual fund tha... ...to produce the same re... ...t investors would get if th... ...ed all the stocks in a p... ...r stock index, often the Standard and Poor's 500 stock index.

Indexing: Buying and holding a mix of stocks that match the performance of a broad stock-market barometer such as the Standard & Poor's 500 stock index.

Index option: An agreement that gives an investor the right but not the obligation to buy or sell the basket of stocks represented by a stock-market index at a specific price on or before a specific date. Index options allow investors to trade in a particular market or industry group without having to buy all the stocks individually.

Individual Retirement Account (IRA): A tax-deferred plan that can help build a retirement nest egg. Individuals whose income is less than a certain amount or who are not active participants in an employer's retirement plan generally can deduct some or all of their annual IRA contributions when figuring their income tax. Others can make nondeductible IRA contributions.

Inflation: A sustained rise in prices in an economy.

Initial public offering (IPO): The first time a company issues stock to the public. This process often is called "going public."

Insider: A person, such as an executive or director, who has information about a company before the information is available to the public.

Insider trading: In one respect, it refers to the legal trading of securities by corporate officers based on information available to the public. In another respect, it refers to the illegal trading of securities by any investor based on information not available to the public.

Instinet: An electronic securities broker through which large institutional firms and broker-dealers can trade stocks.

Intermediate-term bonds: Bonds that mature in five to ten years.

International Monetary Fund (IMF): An organization that makes loans and provides other services intended to stabilize world currencies and promote orderly and balanced trade. Member nations may obtain foreign currency when needed, making it possible to make adjustments in their balance of payments without currency depreciation.

In-the-money: A term used to describe an option that is worth something if exercised immediately. In the case of a call option, it means the current price is higher than the strike price. In the case of a put option, it means the current price is below the strike price.

Investment grade: An assessment of a debt issue by a credit-rating firm that indicates investors are expected to receive principal and interest payments in full and on time.

J

Junior security: A security that has lower priority in claims on assets and income than other securities.

Junk bonds: High-yield bonds that credit-rating agencies consider speculative. The bonds typically offer higher yields and carry higher risk than bonds with investment-grade ratings.

K

Keogh plan: A tax-deferred retirement-savings plan for small-business owners or self-employed people who have earned income from their trade or business. Contributions to the Keogh plan are tax deductible.

Kiddie tax: Special tax treatment for investment earnings of children under the age of 14.

L

Leading economic indicators: A composite of 10 economic indicators developed to help forecast changes in the economy. The indicators are: money supply, unemployment claims, interest rate spreads, average workweek, consumer expectations, stock prices, building permits, vendor performance, manufacturers' new orders for capital goods and manufacturers' new orders for consumer goods.

Leverage: The use of borrowed assets by a business to enhance the return on the owner's equity. The expectation is that the interest rate charged will be lower than the earnings made on the money. In securities markets, leverage refers to money borrowed to cover part of the cost of a purchase.

Leveraged buyout: The purchase of a company by a small group of investors financed largely by debt, often in the form of junk bonds.

Liabilities: The claims against a corporation or other entity. They include accounts payable, wages and salaries, dividends, taxes, and obligations such as bonds, debentures, and bank loans.

Limit order: An order to be filled only at a certain price, or better.

Liquidation: The process of converting stock or other assets into cash. When a company is liquidated, the cash obtained is first used to pay debts and obligations to holders of bonds and preferred stock. Whatever cash remains is distributed on a per-share basis to the holders of common stock.

Liquidity: The ease of converting an asset to cash.

Load: Sales charges on mutual funds and mutual-fund trading.

Load funds: Mutual funds that charge a sales commission, as opposed to no-load funds, which do not levy a fee when you buy or sell. Some fund groups that sell directly to the public offer low-load funds, which charge an upfront fee of 2 percent or 3 percent, but most load funds are sold by brokers.

Long-term bonds: Bonds with maturities of more than ten years.

Long-term debt: Debt that must be paid in a year or more.

Long-term Equity Anticipation Securities (LEAPS): Options that won't expire for up to three years. A registered trademark of the Chicago Board Options Exchange.

M

Major Market Index: This stock index encompasses 20 blue-chip stocks, including 17 that are also in the Dow Jones Industrial Average. Options and futures are based on this index.

Margin: In the stock market, the amount of cash that must be put up in a purchase of securities. If the margin requirement is 50 percent, the buyer must put up 50 percent of the purchase price; the buyer must borrow the rest.

Margin account: A brokerage account allowing customers to buy securities with money borrowed from the brokerage.

Marginal tax rate: The tax rate you would owe on your next dollar of taxable income. This can be highly valuable information when you are making investment decisions.

Margin call: A demand upon an investor to put up more collateral for securities bought on credit. The lender, usually the brokerage firm, makes the call when the equity in the investor's account falls below the level set by the brokerage.

Margin rate: A constant value added to the index rate of an adjustable-rate mortgage to compute the current interest rate.

Market capitalization: The total market value of a company or stock. Market capitalization is calculated by multiplying the number of shares by the current market price of the shares.

Market maker: In a stock market, a trader responsible for maintaining an orderly market in an individual stock by standing ready to buy or sell shares. On a stock exchange, a market maker is known as a specialist.

Market timing: Shifting money in and out of investment markets in an effort to take advantage of rising prices and avoid being stung by downturns. Few, if any, investors manage to be consistently successful in timing markets.

Match trading: Stock transactions made outside of an auction or negotiation process. Buy and sell orders for the same security, at the same price, are paired and executed, often by computer.

Maturity date: When a bond expires and the loan must be paid back in full.

Medicaid: The government program that provides health-care assistance to the poor.

Medicare: The government program that provides health-care assistance for older and disabled people.

Money market account: A federally insured account available at many banks, credit unions, and savings and loan associations.

Money market fund: A type of mutual fund that invests in stable, short-term securities. Money funds are easily convertible into cash, but are not insured by the federal government.

Money supply: Total amount of money made up of currency-in-circulation and checking and savings accounts at banks and savings and loan associations.

Mortgage-backed securities: Debt issues backed by a

pool of mortgages. Investors receive payments from the interest and principal payments made on the underlying mortgages.

Mortgage bonds: Debt issues secured by a mortgage on the issuer's property, such as buildings or equipment.

Municipal bonds: Bonds issued by local government authorities, including states, cities, and their agencies.

Mutual fund: A fund that pools the money of its investors to buy a variety of securities. Open-end mutual funds sell as many shares as investors want. Closed-end mutual funds offer only a fixed number of shares and usually trade on an exchange.

Mutual fund supermarket: Rather than limiting itself to a particular fund family, a supermarket offers one-stop shopping for funds from various fund families.

N

Naked: An investment strategy in which the seller does not own the underlying security.

Nasdaq: An electronic stock market run by the National Association of Securities Dealers. Brokers get price quotes through a computer network and trade via telephone or computer network.

Nasdaq Composite Index: An index that covers the price movements of all stocks traded on the Nasdaq Stock Market.

Nasdaq National Market: A subdivision of the Nasdaq Stock Market that contains the largest and most actively traded stocks on Nasdaq. Companies must meet more stringent standards to be included in this section than they do to be included in the other major subdivision, the Nasdaq Small-Cap Market.

National Association of Investors Corporation: A group that provides information, education, and other services on setting up and operating a successful investment club.

National Association of Securities Dealers (NASD): A membership organization for securities-brokerage firms and underwriters in the U.S. It sets guidelines for ethics and standardized industry practices, and has a disciplinary structure for looking into allegations of rules violations. The NASD also operates the Nasdaq Stock Market.

Net asset value (NAV): For a mutual fund, the NAV is the value of all investments held by the fund, usually expressed in per-share terms. The NAV is calculated daily at the close of the markets.

Net income: The amount left after a company's taxes and all other expenses have been paid. Also called earnings or profit.

Net worth: The amount by which assets exceed liabilities.

New York Stock Exchange (NYSE): The largest U.S. stock market in terms of capitalization. The total market value of roughly 2,300 companies whose shares are listed there is about $5 trillion. It was founded in 1792.

Nikkei: There are several Nikkei indexes. Most often it refers to the index that is the daily average of 225 large-capitalization stocks on the Tokyo Stock Exchange.

No-load mutual fund: A type of mutual fund that sells its shares at market value without sales charges.

Note: A written promise by a government or corporation to repay a debt on an agreed upon date.

NYSE composite index: An index that covers the price movements of all stocks listed on the New York Stock Exchange.

O

Odd lot: Purchase or sale of securities in any amount less than 100 shares.

Open-end mutual fund: A type of fund that issues as many shares as investors demand. Most mutual funds are open-end funds.

Open interest: A measure of liquidity in futures and options. Open interest is the total number of futures contracts or options that have been opened with either a purchase or a sale and not yet closed by an offsetting opposite purchase or sale.

Operating income: Net income excluding income derived from sources other than the company's regular activities and before income deductions. Also called net operating income or net operating loss.

Options: Convey the right, but not the obligation, to buy or sell an underlying security or commodity during a specific time for a specific price. Options are traded on several exchanges, including the Chicago Board of Options Exchange, the American Stock Exchange, the Philadelphia Stock Exchange, the Pacific Stock Exchange, and the New York Stock Exchange.

Option series: A number of options on the same underlying stock that have the same strike price and expiration month.

Out-of-the-money: A term used to describe an option worth nothing if exercised immediately. In the case of a call option, it means the strike price is higher than the current price of the underlying security. In the case of a put option, it means the strike price is lower than the current price of the underlying security.

Over-the-counter (OTC) derivative: A financial contract, whose value is designed to track the return on stocks, bonds, currencies or some other benchmark, that is traded over-the-counter or off organized exchanges, and usually by telephone.

Over-the-counter market: A market in which securities transactions are conducted by dealers through a telephone and computer network connecting dealers in stocks and bonds. Also called OTC trading.

Over-the-counter (OTC) securities: Securities which trade via dealers through negotiation of price rather than through the use of an auction system such as on a stock exchange.

P

Par value: The face value of a security.

Payment date: The date on which a stock's dividend or a bond's interest payment is scheduled to be paid.

Payout ratio: The percentage of earnings paid to shareholders as dividends.

Penny stocks: Many penny stocks do indeed have a share price of less than $1, but this informal designation now often includes stocks that are priced at $5 and below.

Personal Financial Specialist: Financial planning designation given to qualifying accountants by the American Institute of Certified Public Accountants, based in New York.

Pink Sheets: Daily listing of prices of OTC securities not traded on the Nasdaq. Published by the National Quotation Bureaus Inc on pink paper. Now available electronically on the OTC Bulletin Board.

Ponzi scheme: A fraudulent scheme. It is a specific form of pyramiding in which money paid by later investors or contributors is used to pay inflated returns to earlier investors—until the funds dry up because no more contributors can be found.

Portability: Term that means you can roll over all the proceeds from one 401k into another plan when you change jobs.

Portfolio: A collection of securities held by an investor.

Portfolio insurance: A method of hedging, or protecting, the value of a stock portfolio by selling stock-index futures contracts when the stock market declines. The practice was a major contributor to the October 1987 stock market crash.

Precious metals: Commodities such as gold and silver that are used as investment instruments.

Preferred stock: Shares of a company that have no voting rights but do have a set, guaranteed dividend payment. Preferred stockholders are entitled to receive their money before common stockholders in the event of company liquidation.

Premium: In general, the amount by which one security price exceeds another security price.

Price/Sales Ratio (P/S): A stock price measured against a company's sales.

Price-to-book ratio (P/B): A company's stock price divided by its per-share book value. If a company's stock is trading below book value, that may mean the shares are undervalued.

Price-to-earnings ratio (P/E): A ratio to evaluate a stock's worth. It is calculated by dividing the stock's price by an earnings-per-share figure. If calculated with the past year's earnings, it is called the trailing P/E. If calculated with an analyst's forecast for next year's earnings, it is called a forward P/E. Also called the P/E ratio or multiple.

Pricing: The job of the underwriter to determine the offering price for a sale of securities to investors.

Prime rate: The interest rate banks charge their most credit-worthy commercial customers. Banks use the prime as a base to set rates for credit cards, home-equity loans, and other loans, including loans to small- and medium-sized businesses.

Private placement: The sale of stocks or other investments directly to an investor. The securities in a private placement don't have to be registered with the Securities and Exchange Commission.

Profit: The amount left after a company's taxes and all other expenses have been paid. Also called net income or earnings.

Profit margin: A measure of a company's profitability, cost structure, and efficiency, calculated by dividing profits by sales. Gross profit margins are based on gross profits—sales minus the cost of producing the goods sold. Pretax profit margins are based on pretax profits—sales minus all operating expenses. After-tax profit margins are based on after-tax profits—sales minus operating expenses and taxes.

Profit-sharing plan: A retirement plan funded by employer contributions that are based on a share of the company's profits. Employees are frequently responsible for managing the money themselves, selecting from such investments as mutual funds, company stock, and guaranteed investment contracts. Investment gains are not taxed until the money is withdrawn.

Profit-taking: Selling securities after a recent, often rapid price increase.

Program trading: Stock trades involving the purchase or sale of a basket including 15 or more stocks with a total market value of $1 million or more. Most program trades are executed on the New York Stock Exchange, using computerized trading systems. Index arbitrage is the most prominently reported type of program trading.

Prospectus: A formal, written offer to sell securities that sets forth the plan for a proposed or existing business. The prospectus must be filed with the Securities and Exchange Commission and given to prospective buyers. A prospectus includes information on a company's finances, risks, products, services, and management.

Proxy: Written authorization given by a shareholder to someone else to vote on the shareholder's behalf at the company's annual meeting.

Proxy fight: A contest for control of a company in which one or more companies, groups, or individuals seek proxies from a company's shareholders to back a takeover attempt.

Proxy statement: A document mailed with a proxy that gives information about the company or group seeking the proxy votes and matters scheduled for consideration at the shareholder meeting.

Public company: A company that sells shares of its stock to the public. Public companies are regulated by the Securities and Exchange Commission. Also called a publicly held company.

Put option: An agreement that gives an investor the right but not the obligation to sell a stock, bond, commodity, or other instrument at a specified price within a specific time period.

Q

Qualitative analysis: A research technique that deals with factors that cannot be precisely measured such as employee morale and management expertise.

Quant: Slang reference to an analyst who uses quantitative research techniques.

Quantitative analysis: A research technique that deals with measurable items such as the value of assets and the cost of capital.

Quote: A price quotation made up of both the bid and the ask price for a security at a given time.

R

Real Estate Investment Trusts (REITs): A trust or association that invests in a variety of real estate. REITs are managed by one or more trustees, like a mutual fund, and trade like a stock. No federal income tax needs to be paid by the trust if 75 percent of the income is real-estate related and 95 percent of the income is distributed to investors. Individual investors can be taxed.

Receivables: Found on the balance and income statement, this is what customers owe the company.

Recession: A downturn in economic activity, broadly defined by many economists as at least two consecutive quarters of decline in a nation's gross domestic product.

Record date: The date on which a shareholder must own a company's stock to be entitled to receive a dividend.

Recovery: In a business cycle, the period after a downturn or recession when economic activity picks up and the gross domestic product increases.

Regional exchanges: Securities exchanges located outside of New York City. They include the Boston, Philadelphia, Chicago, Cincinnati, and Pacific stock exchanges. Stocks listed on the New York Stock Exchange or the American Stock Exchange also may trade on regional exchanges.

Registered investment advisor: Someone who has

received approval from the Securities and Exchange Commission to give financial advice to clients for a fee.

Registered representative: The official term for a stockbroker or account executive with a brokerage firm.

Repurchase agreement: An agreement between a bank and an investor for the bank to borrow money from the investor for a short time, usually less than 90 days. Repurchase agreements are widely used on the money market by governments' central banks. Also called a repo or buyback.

Return on equity: A measure of how much the company earns on the investment of its shareholders. It is calculated by dividing a company's net income by its common shareholders' equity.

Return on investment: A measure of how much the company earns on the money the company itself has invested. It is calculated by dividing the company's net income by its net assets.

Revenue: Money a company takes in, including interest earned and receipts from sales, services provided, rents, and royalties.

Revenue bond: A bond backed only by revenue from the airport, roadway or other facility that was built with the money it raised.

Rights offering: Offering of rights to existing shareholders of a company to additional shares, usually at a discount to the market price. The shares can be actively traded.

Roth IRAs: As opposed to traditional IRAs that tax withdrawals, all proceeds from Roth IRAs may be withdrawn tax-free. They also have more liberal deposit guidelines.

Round lots: 100-share increments of stock.

Russell 2000: A small-capitalization stock index. It consists of the 2,000 smallest securities in the Russell 3000.

S

Secondary market: Market for issues that were previously offered or sold.

Secondary offering: The sale to the public of a usually large block of stock that is owned by an existing shareholder.

Sector funds: Mutual funds that invest in a single-industry sector, such as biotechnology, gold, or regional banks. Sector funds tend to generate erratic performance, and they often dominate both the top and bottom of the annual mutual fund performance charts.

Securities and Exchange Commission (SEC): The federal agency that enforces securities laws and sets standards for disclosure about publicly traded securities, including mutual funds. It was created in 1934 and consists of five commissioners appointed by the president and confirmed by the senate to staggered terms.

Securities Investor Protection Corporation (SIPC): The nonprofit corporation that insures the securities and cash in the customer accounts of brokerage firms up to $500,000 in the event a firm fails. All brokers and dealers registered with the Securities and Exchange Commission are required to be members.

Security: A financial instrument that indicates the holder owns a share or shares of a company (stock) or has loaned money to a company or government organization (bond).

Sell-off: A period of intensified selling in a market that pushes prices sharply lower.

Share: An investment that represents part ownership of a company or a mutual fund.

Short: Buying and then selling securities that one does not own, expecting a drop in prices.

Short covering: Trades that reverse, or close out, short-sale positions. In the stock market, for instance, shares are purchased to replace the shares previously borrowed.

Short interest: Total number of shares of a given stock that have been sold short and not yet repurchased.

Short-term gain or loss: For tax purposes, the profit or loss from selling capital assets or securities held six months or less. Short-term gains are taxed at the highest ordinary income-tax rate.

Simplified Employee Pension (SEP): A retirement plan for the self-employed that is also referred to as a SEP-IRA.

Small-capitalization stocks: Shares of relatively small publicly traded corporations, typically with a total market value, or capitalization, of less than $600 million. Also called small-cap stocks or small caps.

Socially responsible funds: These funds stick to companies that they deem to be of reputable social value. That means some funds will avoid investing in companies dealing in nuclear power, alcohol, or tobacco.

Specialist: A stock exchange member who is designated to maintain a fair and orderly market in a specific stock. He is required to buy and sell for his own account to counteract temporary imbalances in supply and demand.

Spin-off: The distribution to a company's shareholders of the stock in a division or subsidiary.

Split: This represents a division of an existing stock. For instance, if a company declares a 2-for-1 split, this effectively divides the stock price in half.

Spot market: A market for buying or selling commodities or foreign exchange for immediate delivery and for cash payment.

Spot price: The price of a commodity or currency available for immediate sale and delivery.

Spread: In stocks, the difference between the bid and asked prices. In fixed-income securities, the difference between the yields on securities of the same quality but different maturity or the difference between the yields on securities of the same maturity but of different quality.

Stagflation: The combination of high inflation and slow economic growth.

Standard & Poor's 500 stock index: A benchmark index of 500 large stocks, maintained by Standard & Poor's, a division of McGraw-Hill Co. Also called the S&P 500.

Stock: An investment that represents part ownership of a company. There are two different types of stock: common and preferred. Common stocks provide voting rights but no guarantee of dividend payments. Preferred stocks provide no voting rights but have a set, guaranteed dividend payment. Also called shares.

Stock appreciation rights: An executive compensation plan, usually linked to stock options, that gives recipients the opportunity to benefit from a rise in the company's stock price without exercising the options. Stock-appreciation-rights payments can be in cash, an equivalent amount of stock or some combination of the two.

Stock-index futures: A contract to buy or sell the cash value of a stock index by a specified date.

Stock-index option: An agreement that gives its holder

the right, but not the obligation, to buy or sell a specified amount of an underlying investment—a stock-index futures contract or the cash value of a stock index—by a given date at a given price.

Stock option: An agreement allowing an investor to buy or sell stock within a stipulated time and for a certain price. Also, it is a method of employee compensation that gives workers the right to buy the company's stock during a specified period of time at a stipulated exercise price.

Stop order: An investor's order to a broker to buy or sell a security when its market price reaches a certain level.

Straddling: An investor buys a call and a put on the same underlying investment.

Strike price: A specified price at which an investor can buy or sell an option's underlying security.

Strip: The practice of splitting a bond's principal and coupon (the interest rate that the bond issuer's promises to pay) and then selling them separately. The Treasury issues one variation, known as Strips, an acronym for Separate Trading of Registered Interest and Principal of Securities.

Subordinated debenture: A debt security that will be paid off after the issuer first pays off debt to senior creditors in the event of the dissolution of the company.

SuperDOT: An electronic system used to route buy and sell orders to the floor of the New York Stock Exchange. Among other things, it is used to execute computerized program trades. SuperDOT handles about 80 percent of all orders entered at the exchange. DOT is an acronym for Designated Order Turnaround.

Swap: An investor sells one security and simultaneously buys another.

T

Technical analysis: Research of a security or market sector that uses trading data, such as volume and price trends, to make predictions.

Ticks: The smallest allowable movement in the price of a security or index. A downtick is the sale of a security at a price below the preceding deal. An uptick is a sale executed at a price higher than the preceding sale.

Tokyo Stock Price Index: Index of the larger issues on the Tokyo Stock Exchange. Also called TOPIX.

Total return: Annual gains or losses on an investment, reflecting dividends, interest, and price fluctuation.

Traders: People who negotiate prices and execute buy and sell orders, either on behalf of an investor or for their own account.

Trading Curbs: One of several "circuit breakers" adopted by the NYSE and approved by the Securities and Exchange Commission in response to the big market decline in October 1987.

Treasuries: Securities (notes or bills) issued by the U.S. government. A Treasury bill is a certificate representing a short-term loan to the federal government that matures in 3 or 6 months. A Treasury note matures in 2 to 10 years.

Triple-witching hour: Slang for the quarterly expiration of stock-index futures, stock-index options and options on individual stocks. Trading associated with the expirations inflates stock market volume and can cause volatility in prices. Occurs on the third Friday of March, June, September, and December.

Turnover: In accounting terms, the number of times an asset is replaced during a set period. In trading, the volume of shares traded on the exchange on a given day. In employment matters, turnover refers to the total number of employees divided by the number of employees replaced during a certain period. In the U.K., the term refers to a company's annual sales volume.

U

Underwriter: In the securities business, a company that for a fee brings an issue of stocks, bonds, or other securities to market. The underwriter buys all or most of the issue, then resells it to investors.

Uniform Gifts to Minors Act *and* Uniform Transfers to Minors Act: Accounts governed by these acts allow a minor child to own property. The account is managed by a custodian until the child reaches the age of majority. State law determines both the type of account and the age when the child gains control of the assets.

Unit Investment Trust: A fixed portfolio of stocks or bonds with a specific maturity date. Generally sold by brokers.

U.S. savings bonds: Series EE savings bonds are issued by the federal government and sold by most banks, credit unions, and savings and loan associations. They also are available through payroll-deduction plans offered by many employers. Interest is exempt from state and local taxes.

V

Value averaging: A variation on dollar-cost averaging. Instead of investing the same amount of money every time, each investment is adjusted to a prearranged schedule.

Value investing: Value investors are the stock market's bargain hunters. They often lean toward beaten-down companies whose shares appear cheap when compared to current earnings or corporate assets. Value investors typically buy stocks with high dividend yields, or ones that trade at a low price-to-earnings ratio or low price-to-book value.

Value Line Composite Index: A gauge that covers about 1,700 stocks tracked by the Value Line Investment Survey that are traded on the New York Stock Exchange, the Nasdaq Stock Market, and the American Stock Exchange.

Vesting: With regard to 401ks, this is the time allowed before company matching contributions actually become the employee's property.

Volatility: The characteristic of a security or market to fall or rise sharply in price in a short-term period.

Volume: Number of shares traded in a company or an entire market during a given period.

W

Warrant: A security that allows an investor to purchase an amount of stock at a specified price within a certain time period.

Wilshire 5000 Stock Index: Broadest index covering Nasdaq Stock Market stocks and all stocks traded on all the New York Stock Exchange and American Stock Exchange. It is a market-value weighted index.

Wrap account: An investment plan that wraps together money management and brokerage services. Wrap plans are popular for their simplicity. For one all-inclusive annual fee, an investment firm provides the services of a professional money manager who creates a portfolio of stocks and bonds, or mutual funds, and takes care of all the trading.

Writer: In the options market, the seller of put and call options.

Y

Yield: The annual rate of return on an investment, as paid in dividends or interest. It is expressed as a percentage, generally obtained by dividing the current market price for a stock or bond into the annual dividend or interest payment.

Yield curve: The relationship, plotted on a graph, between yield and maturity among bonds of different maturities and the same credit quality, most often Treasuries. A normal or positive yield curve slopes upwards, with short-term rates lower than long-term rates, while an inverted yield curve is the opposite and slopes downwards.

Yield to maturity: Rate of return on a bond if held to maturity. The formula includes the market price, principal paid at maturity, coupon rate and years remaining until maturity.

Z

Zero-coupon bond: A bond sold at a deep discount. It does not pay periodic interest payments to investors; instead, investors receive their return on investment at maturity.

After-hours trading, 96-97, 138
Aggressive growth funds, 54
Allowances, 26
Alternative Minimum Tax, 89, 128
American College, 95
American Depository Receipts (ADRs), 99
American Express, 93
American Stock Exchange, 21, 58
American-style options, 141
Ameritrade, 93
Analysts, 31
Annual reports, 24, 25, 26, 65
Arbitrage, 109
Asset allocation, 18-19
Asset size, of mutual fund, 64
ATM transactions, 111, 145
At the money, 109
Automatic investment programs
    401k account as, 86-87
    in mutual funds, 67, 75
    in stocks, 36-37
Automatic reinvestment, with CDs, 77

Back load, 62
Balanced funds, 54
Balance sheet, 26-27
Banking services, shopping for, 145
Bankrate Monitor, 77, 115
Bear funds (short funds), 32, 33, 58
Beneficiary, of IRA, 79, 80-81
Blend funds, 57
Bond funds, 70-73, 128, 129
Bonds, 14, 42-51
    and asset allocation, 18-19
    in balanced funds, 54
    call provisions, 48, 50
    compared to bond funds, 128
    corporate bonds, 42, 44-45
    debentures, 128
    features of, 42
    general obligation bonds, 45
    how to buy, 50-51
    how to track, 51
    and interest rates, 17, 43, 46-47, 48
    and investment goals, 47
    junk bonds, 44, 45, 46
    laddering, 50
    letter ratings, 44-45
    meaning of, 42
    municipal bonds, 42, 43, 45, 128

revenue bonds, 45
    risks of, 43, 48-49
    savings bonds, 129
    secondary market for, 45
    tax-free, 42, 43, 47, 128
    term of, 42, 43, 46-47
    Treasury bonds, 42-43, 45, 49, 51, 129
    types of, 42-43, 44-45
    useful terms, 44
    yield of, 43, 45, 49, 51
    zero coupon bonds, 45, 129
Breach of contract, 91
Brokers and brokerage houses, 34-35
    client disputes with, 91
    day-trading houses, 101
    discount brokers, 35, 50, 92-93
    online brokers, 35, 66, 92-93, 136-37
    and other professionals, 136
    purchasing mutual funds through, 66
    purchasing zero coupons through, 129
    Registered Representatives, 95
    role in after-hours trading, 96
    traditional (full-service) brokers, 34-35, 50, 90-91, 92, 93
Budgeting, 110-11
Buffett, Warren, 31

Calamos Growth A Fund, 67
Call options, 106, 107, 109
Call provisions, of bonds, 48, 50
Capital gains, 21
Capitalization (market cap), 23. See also Company size
Cash
    and asset allocation, 18-19
    in financial statement, 26
    paying with, 111
Certificates of deposit (CDs), 73, 76-77, 132-33
Certified Financial Planner (CFP), 95
Certified Financial Planner Board of Standards, 95
Certified Public Accountant (CPA), 95
Chartered Financial Analyst (CFA), 95
Chartered Financial Consultant (ChFC), 95

Chat boards, 136-37
Checking accounts, 73, 145
Chicago Board Options Exchange, 140
Churning, 91
Clinton, Hillary, 104
Closed-end funds, 64-65, 72
Closing costs, 114
CNBC Market Watch, 28
CNBC television, 25, 108
Coast-to-Coast Club, 102
Collaborative funds (collective intelligence funds), 59
Collar, 141
College
    as an investment goal, 12-13
    investment scenarios, 19
    saving for, 13, 116-17
College Board Online, 13
Commodities, 104-7
    futures contracts, 104-5, 140
    and options, 106-7
    precious metals funds, 59
Commodity Futures Trading Commission (CFTC), 140
Common stock, 20
Company size (market cap), as fund focus, 56, 57
Compounding, 14, 15, 77
Corporate bond funds, 70
Corporate bonds, 42, 44-45
Cost efficiency, of mutual funds, 52-53
Cost of sales, 27
Coupon rate, 44, 51
Coverdell Education Savings Accounts (CESAs), 84-85
Credit card debt, 112-13
Credit insurance, 125
Credit risk, of bonds, 48
Currency hedging, 98
Currency risk, 99
Current assets, 26
Current liabilities, 26
Current yield, of bonds, 51
Cyclical stocks, 23

Davis Financial A Fund, 67
Day trading, 100-101
Death benefit
    with life insurance, 119
    with variable annuity, 135
Debentures, 128
Debit cards, 111, 113
Dell Computers, 41
Derivatives, 106. See also Futures contracts; Options
Direct purchase
    of bonds, 50
    of mutual funds, 66
    of stocks, 36
Direct purchase plans (DPPs), 36
Disability insurance, 124

Discount bond, 44
Discount brokers, 35, 50, 92-93
Disease-specific insurance, 125
Diversification, 14, 126
    with bond funds, 70
    of bond holdings, 50
    with bonds, 47
    and interest rate effects, 17
    with international funds, 99
    in IRAs, 85
    with mutual funds, 52
    sample portfolios, 18-19
Dividend reinvestment plans (DRIPs), 36
Dividend yield, 29
Dollar-cost averaging, 36-37, 67
Dow Jones Industrial Average (DJIA), 15, 17, 21, 53, 55, 108
Down payment, 114
Dwelling coverage, 122

Early withdrawal penalties
    certificates of deposit, 76, 77
    401k accounts, 87
    IRAs, 79
Earnings per share (EPS), 27
Earthquake insurance, 123
Education IRAs, 84-85, 117
Electronic Communications Networks (ECNs), 96, 97
Emergency fund, 18
Emerging markets, 98
Employee stock options, 88-89
EPS diluted, 27
EPS primary, 27
Equity-linked CDs, 133
Etrade, 93
European-style options, 141
Exchange traded funds (ETFs), 58
Exercise price, of stock option, 88
Expenses, of mutual funds, 53, 61, 62-63, 72
Expiration date, of stock option, 88
Extended-hours trading, 96-97, 138

Face value, 44
Failure to supervise, 91
Family Limited Partnership, 143
Federal Deposit Insurance Corporation (FDIC), 76
Federal Housing Administration (FHA), 114
Federal Reserve, 17
Fee for service plans, 120-21
Fence, 141
Fidelity, 65
Fidelity Select Financial Services Fund, 67
Fidelity Select Home Finance Fund, 67
FinanCenter, 13
Financial planners, 94-95, 136
Financial statements, 26-27

529 College Savings Plans, 116-17
Flight insurance, 125
Float, 20
Flood insurance, 123
Foreign bond funds, 70
Foreign stocks, 99
401k plans, 86-87
    advantages and drawbacks, 86-87
    delayed employer deposits, 144
    power of, 87
    rolling a SEP-IRA into, 142-43
    and variable annuities, 135
403b plans, 87
Frankfurt stock exchange, 138
Front load, 62
Full-service brokers, 34-35, 50, 90-
    91, 92, 93
Fundamental analysis, 30
Fund families, 64, 65
Funds of funds, 59
Futures contracts, 104-5
    commodities futures, 104-5
    hedging vs. speculating, 140
    and options, 106-7
    stock index futures, 108-9

General obligation bonds, 45
Global funds, 138-39
Government bond funds, 70, 73
Grant date, 88
Great Depression, 14
Green funds, 58-59
Greenspan, Alan, 17
Growth and income funds, 55
Growth funds, 54-55, 57
Growth stocks, 22
Guaranteed replacement coverage,
    122

Health insurance, 120-21
Health maintenance organizations
    (HMOs), 121
Hedge funds, 59
Hedging
    compared to speculating, 140
    in foreign currency, 98
High yield bonds. See Junk bonds
Home buying, 114-15
    as an investment goal, 13
    investment scenarios, 19
    online calculator, 13
    ways to amass a down payment,
        114
Home equity line of credit, 113
Home office, insurance for, 124
Homeowner's insurance, 122-23

Incentive stock options, 89
Income flow
    with bond funds, 71
    with bonds, 47
Income statement, 26-27

Income stocks, 22-23
Income tax, in financial statements,
    27
Indexes, 21
    NAIC Top 100, 103
    S&P 500, 21, 33, 55, 58, 108,
        133
    Wilshire 5,000, 21
Index funds, 55, 57
Individual Retirement Accounts
    (IRAs), 78-85
    beneficiary feature, 79, 80-81
    choosing between traditional and
        Roth IRAs, 82-83
    contribution limitations, 78-79,
        80
    converting from a traditional to a
        Roth IRA, 81, 82-83
    Education IRAs, 84-85, 117
    investing checklist, 85
    Roth IRAs, 78, 79, 80-81, 82-83,
        85
    Simplified Employee Pension
        Retirement Accounts (SEP-
        IRAs), 84, 85, 134, 142-43
    Spousal Deductible IRAs, 134
    tax impacts of, 79, 81, 82, 83, 84
    trading investments in, 134
    traditional IRAs, 78-79
    and variable annuities, 135
    withdrawal guidelines, 78, 79, 80,
        81
    withdrawing a down payment
        from, 114
Inflation, 16, 17, 48-49
Initial public offerings (IPOs), 21,
    38-39, 130
Insider trading, 40-41
Instinet Group, 39
Institute of Chartered Financial
    Analysts, 95
Insurance, 118-25
    credit insurance, 125
    disability insurance, 124
    earthquake insurance, 123
    flood insurance, 123
    health insurance, 120-21
    homeowner's insurance, 122-23
    life insurance, 118-19
    unnecessary types, 125
Interest-bearing checking accounts,
    73, 145
Interest payback, bond feature, 42
Interest rate risk
    with certificates of deposit, 77
    with bonds, 43, 46-47, 48
Interest rates, 17
    and bond value, 43, 46-47, 48
    and income stocks, 22
    of money market funds, 74, 75
Internal Revenue Service (IRS), 86,
    128, 143

International funds, 56, 99, 138-39
International investing, 98-99, 138-39
International stocks, 23, 99
In the money, 109
Investment choices, 14
Investment clubs, 102-3
Investment goals, 12-13
    budgeting for, 110-11
    college as, 12-13
    housing as, 13
    retirement as, 12
    reducing risk necessary to
        achieve, 126
    reviewing progress toward, 127
Investment-grade bonds, 44
Investment feature of life insurance,
    118
Investment planning, 12-19, 126-27
    online tools, 13, 137
Investment scenarios, 19
Investment strategy factors, 14-17
    compounding, 14, 15
    diversification, 14
    inflation, 16
    interest rates, 17
    for IRAs, 85
    market volatility, 16-17
    risk tolerance, 14-15
    time and risk, 15

Junk bonds (high yield bonds), 44,
    45, 46

Keogh Plans, 134

Laddering, 50, 133
Large-cap funds, 57
Large caps, 23
Liability insurance, 122-23
Lifecycle mutual funds, 130
Life insurance, 118-19, 125
Limit orders, 33, 96, 97
Liquidity
    of bond funds, 71
    of money market funds, 74
    as a risk of bonds, 48, 49
Load calculator, 63
Loads, 61, 62, 63, 73, 131
Long, 104
Long-Term Equity Anticipation
    Security (LEAP), 140
Lynch, Peter, 31

Major medical insurance, 120
Margin, buying on, 32-33
    and day trading, 100, 101
    exchange traded funds, 58
    futures contracts, 104-5
Margin calls, 33, 105
Market capitalization (market cap),
    23, 57

Market neutral funds, 131
Market volatility, 16-17
Massachusetts Investors Trust, 53
Matures date, of bonds, 51
Maturity, of bond fund, 72
Medical savings accounts (MSAs),
    121
Merrill Lynch, 92, 93
Micro-cap funds, 57
Microsoft, 24
Mid-cap funds, 57
Mid caps, 23
Milan stock exchange, 138
Minimum initial investment, 67, 73,
    75
Minimum withdrawal, 75
Money Magazine, 77
Money market account, 73
Money market mutual funds, 14, 74-
    75, 132-33, 145
Moody's bond ratings, 44
Morningstar, 25, 60
Mortgage calculators, 13, 115
Mortgage insurance, 114, 125
Mortgages, 115
Municipal bond funds, 70, 128
Municipal bonds, 42, 43, 45, 128
Mutual funds, 14, 52-75, 130-31
    advantages and drawbacks, 52-53
    aggressive growth funds, 54
    asset size, 64
    automatic investment programs,
        67
    balanced funds, 54
    blend funds, 57
    bond funds, 70-73, 128, 129
    choosing a fund, 60-61
    closed-end funds, 64-65, 72
    collaborative funds (collective
        intelligence funds), 59
    with company size (market cap)
        focus, 56, 57
    compared to variable annuities,
        135
    cost efficiency of, 52-53
    exchange traded funds (ETFs), 58
    expenses of, 53, 61, 62-63, 72
    first fund, 52
    fund families, 64, 65
    funds of funds, 59
    global funds, 138-39
    growth of, 53
    growth and income funds, 55
    growth funds, 54-55, 57
    hedge funds, 59
    how to buy, 66-67
    index funds, 55, 57
    introduction to, 52-53
    international funds, 56, 99, 138-39
    international holdings of, 139
    investment minimums, 67
    lifecycle funds, 130
    loads, 61, 62, 63, 73, 131

management of, 52, 60, 61, 64
market neutral funds, 131
money market funds, 74-75, 132-33
newly issued, 130
performance of, 60, 61, 72
portfolio mix, 61
portfolio turnover, 63, 73
precious metals funds, 59
real estate investment trusts (REITS), 59
research sources, 65, 69
risk of, 60-61, 74
sector funds, 56
short funds (bear funds), 32, 33, 58
socially responsible funds (green funds), 58-59
stock funds, 54-59
tax efficiency of, 63
tax-managed funds, 62
tracking of, 68-69
types of, 54-59
value funds, 57
Mutual fund supermarkets, 66

Naked options, 109
NASDAQ National Market System, 20, 21, 58, 97, 101, 108
National Association of Investors Corporation (NAIC), 102, 103
National Association of Securities Dealers (NASD), 91, 95
National Flood Insurance System, 123
Net asset value (NAV), 68
Net income, 27
New York Stock Exchange, 21
Nokia, 99
No-load funds, 62, 63, 131
Nonqualified stock options, 89

Online brokers, 35, 66, 92-93, 136-37
Online calculators, 13, 63
Online financial-planning tools, 137
Online investment clubs, 102
Online mutual fund data, 65, 69
Open-end funds, 64, 72
Options, 14, 106-7, 108, 109
collars, 141
European- vs. American-style, 141
LEAPs, 140
naked, 109
premiums, 106, 140
Out of the money, 109
Over-the-counter (OTC) market, 20, 21

Penny stocks, 21
Performance
of bond fund, 72

of mutual funds, 53, 60
Pink Sheets, 21
Planner's Uniform Application for Investment Advisor Registration (ADV), 94, 95
Planning, 12-19, 126-27. *See also* Financial planners
Points, 114
Portfolio mix, of mutual fund, 61
Portfolio tracking, 92
Portfolio turnover, 63, 73
Precious metals funds, 59
Preferred provider organizations (PPOs), 121
Preferred stock, 20-21
Premium, for options, 106, 107, 140
Premium bond, 44
Prepaid tuition plans, 116, 117
Pre-tax income, 27
Price-book ratio (P/B), 28-29
Price-earnings ratio (P/E), 28
Price-sales ratio (P/S), 29
Private mortgage insurance (PMI), 114
ProFunds Bear Fund, 33
Property and equipment, 26
Prospectus, 65
Proxy, 21
Prudent Bear Fund, 58
Put options, 106, 107, 109

Qubes, 58

Real estate investment trusts (REITs), 59
Receivables, 26
Registered Investment Advisor, 95
Registered Representative, 95
Renter's insurance, 125
Research data
from analysts, 31
and chat boards, 136-37
from discount brokers, 92
on insider trading, 40
on mutual funds, 65
on stocks, 25
Resistance level, 30
Retirement, as investment goal, 12, 13
Retirement accounts
Keogh Plans, 134
sample portfolios, 19
trading in, 134-35
See also 401k plans; Individual Retirement Accounts (IRAs)
Revenue bonds, 45
Risk
of futures and options, 104, 105, 108
of money market funds, 74
of mutual funds, 60-61
reducing, 126
time and, 15

Risk tolerance, 14-15, 85
Roth, William, 80
Roth IRAs, 78, 79, 80-81, 82-83, 85

Sample portfolios, 18-19
Saving
    on banking services, 145
    and budgeting, 110-11
    for college, 116-17
    on credit card costs, 113
    on insurance costs, 123
    via whole life insurance, 118
Savings
    in bonds, 47
    in money market mutual funds,
        74-75
    paying credit card debt with, 113
    short-term vehicles, 73
Savings accounts, 145
Savings bonds, 129
Schwab, 92, 93, 129
Secondary market, 45
Secondary offerings, 21, 38
Second-to-die insurance, 119
Sector funds, 56
Securities, in financial statement, 26
Securities and Exchange
    Commission (SEC), 40, 91, 95
Short, 104
Short selling, 32, 33
Short-term savings vehicles, 73
Simplified Employee Pension
    Retirement Accounts (SEP-
    IRAs), 84, 85
compared to Keogh Plan, 134
rolling into a 401k, 142-43
and Spousal Deductible IRA, 134
Small-cap funds, 57
Small caps, 23
Smith Barney Aggressive Growth A
    Fund, 67
Smythe, R.M., 142
Socially responsible funds, 58-59
Social Security, 13
Software financial-planning tools,
    137
SPDRs, 58
Speculating, versus hedging, 140
Spousal Deductible IRA, 134
Spreads, 21
Standard and Poor's bond ratings, 44
Standard and Poor's 500 Index, 21,
    33, 55, 58, 108, 133
Standard deviation, 60
Stock analysts, 31
Stockbrokers. See Brokers and broker-
    age houses
Stock buybacks, 139
Stock certificates, old issues, 142
Stock exchanges, 21
Stock indexes. See Indexes
Stock index futures, 108-9
Stock market, volatility of, 16-17

Stock options, 88-89
Stock-picking games, 34
Stocks, 14, 20-41
    after-hours trading, 96-97, 138
    analyzing, evaluating, and choos-
        ing, 23, 24-31
    and asset allocation, 18-19
    average annual return, 20
    buying on margin, 32-33
    categories of, 20-21, 22-23
    common vs. preferred shares, 20-
        21
    cyclical, 23
    data sources, 25
    direct purchase plans (DPPs), 36
    dividend reinvestment plans
        (DRIPs), 36
    dividend yield, 29
    dollar-cost averaging, 36-37
    glossary, 21
    how to buy, 34-37
    initial public offerings, 21, 38-39
    insider trading, 40-41
    and interest rates, 17
    international, 23, 99
    limit orders, 33, 96, 97
    meaning of, 20
    over-the-counter (OTC) trading,
        20
    price-book ratio (P/B), 28-29
    price-earnings ratio (P/E), 28
    price-sales ratio (P/S), 29
    secondary issues, 38
    selling short, 32, 33
    stop loss order, 33
    "systems" for selecting, 30
    special strategies, 32-33
    technical analysis, 30-31
    value averaging, 37
Stock screens, 29, 31
Stock splits, 21
Stop loss order, 33
Straddling, 109
Strike price, 106, 109
Support level, 30

Tax-adjusted return, 63
Tax-efficiency ratio, 63
Taxes
    and employee stock options, 89
    and long-term goals, 127
Tax-free bonds, 42, 43, 47, 70, 128
Tax-free money market funds, 132
Tax-managed funds, 62
Tax planners, 136
Teaser credit cards, 112
Technical analysis, 30-31
Term insurance, 118
Time and risk, 15
Total liabilities, 27
Total revenues, 27
Treasury bills, 42, 45, 47
Treasury bonds, 42, 43, 45, 49, 50,

51, 129
Treasury Direct, 50
Treasury notes, 42, 45
Treasury yield curve, 43

Umbrella insurance, 124-25
Uniform Gift to Minors Accounts
    (UGMAs), 116, 117, 143
Uniform Transfer to Minors
    Accounts (UTMAs), 116, 117
Universal life insurance, 119
Unsuitable trading, 91

Value averaging, 37
Value funds, 57
Value Line, 60
Value stocks, 22
Vanguard Wellington Fund, 61
Variable annuity, 135
Variable life insurance, 119
Vesting, in 401k program, 86-87

Veterans Administration (VA), 114
Volatility
    of IPOs, 39
    of international funds, 99
    of stock market, 16-17

Washington Mutual Investors Fund,
    69
Weighted average maturity, 72
Whole life insurance, 118-19
Wilshire 5,000 Index, 21

Yield
    on bond funds, 72
    on bonds, 42, 43, 45, 51
    on certificates of deposit, 77
    on money market funds, 75
    on stocks, 29
Yield curve, of Treasury bond, 43

Zero-coupon bonds (strips), 45, 129

Glossary

More great books from

CNBC

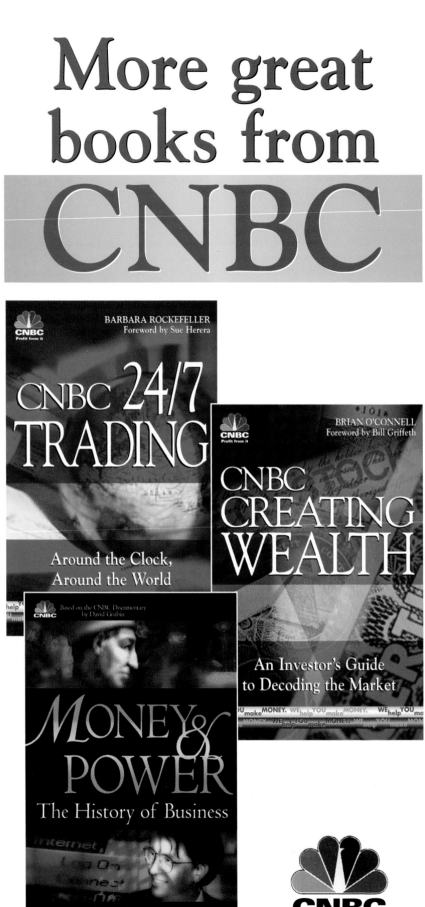

BARBARA ROCKEFELLER
Foreword by Sue Herera

CNBC 24/7 TRADING

Around the Clock,
Around the World

BRIAN O'CONNELL
Foreword by Bill Griffeth

CNBC CREATING WEALTH

An Investor's Guide
to Decoding the Market

Based on the CNBC Documentary
by David Grubin

MONEY & POWER
The History of Business

Howard Means with a Foreword by David Grubin

CNBC
Profit from it